The UNSTOPPABLE WOMAN in BUSINESS

The UNSTOPPABLE WOMAN in BUSINESS

A woman's entrepreneurial blueprint to convert **setbacks** into **solutions** and **strategies** to successfully *STEP* Out, *STAND* Out & *SOAR* in Business

WINSTON CARTIER PUBLISHING

NELLA CHIKWE

WITH

Global Women Leading to *Inspire* and *Influence*

upon financial, professional, psychological, behavioural, relationship or health concerns who may be experiencing any anxiety, depression or stress, should take counsel with an appropriate qualified professional. This anthology is not an alternate solution for enlisting qualified professionals to assist with the reader's specific lifestyle, issues, concerns and/or personal or professional circumstances.

WINSTONCARTIERPUBLISHING.COM

DEDICATION

The Unstoppable Woman In Business series is dedicated to every aspiring conscious woman in business who desires to lead an unstoppable life. Build a legacy, not just a business. For every unstoppable woman to value her worth and carry an abundance mindset with heart, vision and compassion in pursuit to purpose. Focusing on prospering lives as she continues to thrive and profit in business.

I pay tribute to all my contributing co-authors. I commend their family and friends support in having their voice heard!

Thank you to my one and only true love, husband, business and life partner *Julius*. I appreciate your unconditional love, support and encouragement as I fulfil my life's purpose in raising up women leaders to increase their value and influence globally. By allowing their voices to be heard. As their Story Matters!

Savannah Cartier Chikwe, my precious daughter. May this series and the upcoming anthologies continue to inspire your love for literature and creative writing. Thus, allowing the divine words to flow in and through you to touch deeply and inspire greatly; many young teens, young ladies and women around the globe. I know my legacy will live on and you will one day carry the torch.

Jordan Winston Chikwe, my quick-witted son. May the drive, tenaciousness, resilience, determination and unwavering faith that you've witnessed in my pursuit to purpose. Continue to teach you that '*Women's Voices Matter*". As it says in scripture '*I can do all things through Christ who strengthens me.*' Philippians 4:13. YES, women can do all things that they set their minds on and can be the change they want to see. A lasting, empowering and everlasting change!

Who can find a virtuous woman? For her price is far above rubies.

-Proverbs 31:10.

ACKNOWLEDGEMENTS

In all His Glory, I want to acknowledge God; to have chosen me to fulfill His purpose through *The Unstoppable Woman Of Purpose Global Movement*. He has shown up boldly and renewed my strength in releasing this anthology and accompanied workbook; along with publishing a total of four anthologies of a 24-part series out into the world. So, that many women can become an unstoppable woman of purpose.

I offer special thanks to my unstoppable co-authors and women leading to inspire and influence; Sarah Griffiths (Aust), Hazel Todd (Aust), Melissa Brown Odazie (USA) and Veronika Whyte (Aust). Thank you for being the CORE in pioneering this anthology series and supporting the global movement. By sharing their stories, strategies and insights to inspire and influence many aspiring women leaders around the globe. Thank you for what you represent!

I am grateful to my astounding global publishing and marketing team, you know who you are. Thank you for your tremendous support and believing in the global expansive vision. My heart is full of heartfelt gratitude.

"The goal isn't to live forever, is to create something that will."

-Chuck Palahnuik

THE BOOK COVER ARTWORK DESIGN, ELEMENTS & SYMBOLIC MEANINGS

Every thought and attention to detail to the anthology cover have been carefully articulated. Illustrating the essence of the unstoppable woman of purpose and its reflection to the profound written words and stories shared in this global publication.

Brushstroke Background Effect

Represents the unstoppable woman of worth making her mark! The raw brushstroke signifies her own unique beauty and embracing all of her imperfections, as she is uniquely and wonderfully made. It's an element of her expression, true essence and authenticity.

Beautiful Young Woman

Purpose and success doesn't discriminate on age. A woman can have beauty and boldness. Confidence is her best accessory. Success is inevitable with a millionaire mindset, clear purpose, drive, determination, unwavering willpower to never give up and achieve all heights. She can be beautiful and bountiful in her business ventures. Because she is worth it!

Shattered Glass

The shattered glass represents the limitless leader. An unstoppable woman in business smashes the glass ceiling and confidently achieves all of her business goals with tenacity and resilience. She is unscathed by rising above all adversity and still carries poise and dignity in her dealings in business. She is simply unmovable, unbreakable, unshakeable and unapologetically unstoppable.

Woman Wearing Red Lipstick

Red is the new black for the confident woman of worth. She wears it audaciously and knows it represents the power that lies within. Igniting her souls purpose on fire. She is limitless leader and is fierce and fearless in everyway. She is bold in her business practises and embraces her value, vision and voice to be heard. She is daring and willing to step out, stand out and soar in business.

"She was unapologetically unstoppable and unshakeable, not because she did not have any trepidations or doubts. But because she continued to press on despite them."

-Nella Chikwe

THE UNSTOPPABLE WOMAN IN BUSINESS

A Woman's Entrepreneurial Blueprint to Convert Setbacks into Solutions and Strategies to Successfully Step Out, Stand Out and Soar in Business

CONTENTS

INTRODUCTION

IT'S YOUR TIME TO BE UNSTOPPABLE

In "The Unstoppable Woman Of Purpose Global Anthologies Movement' – Volume 2, Nella Chikwe with four global women share their success stories and strategies of being unapologetically unstoppable; stepping out into the world with sheer confidence, courage and certainty.

RECOGNISING THEM: Sarah Griffiths (Aust), Hazel Todd (Aust), Melissa Brown Odazie (USA) and Veronika Whyte (Aust).

In the second instalment of this series of anthologies, women are awakened and equipped with strategies to convert setbacks into successful solutions to confidently step out, stand out and soar in business.

VISIONARY WOMAN, DO YOU...?

- Desire to be more, do more and no longer play small
- Yearn to be unstoppable, fierce and fearless in business
- Turn your purpose into profit

THE INTENTION OF THIS ANTHOLOGY IS TO SHOW YOU

- How to embrace your divine gifts with feminine grace
- Master your millionaire mindset
- Expand and elevate your brand and business
- Value your worth and your message
- Courageously charge your inner power
- Begin the journey of becoming an unstoppable woman in business
- Transform your passion and purpose into profit
- Stand out, step out and soar in business

This is your moment to rise, transform your setbacks into success. Step into your greatness, as it's your birthright. IT'S TIME TO SOAR HIGHER AND MAKE SHIFT HAPPEN!

"Find Your VOICE in Your Story; as Passion Ignites When Purpose Unites."

-Nella Chikwe

UYW

PART I

MELISSA BROWN ODAZIE

"Beautiful girl, you were made to do hard things, so believe in yourself."

- Unknown

YOU'RE NOT HERE BY MISTAKE, YOU WERE MADE FOR THIS

BY MELISSA BROWN ODAZIE

"Beautiful girl, you were made to do hard things, so believe in yourself."

- Unknown

You orchestrate your own life, you are the conductor, and the moment you realize that, that is the moment that it all starts to fall into place. This wasn't always easy for me to grasp, constantly questioning myself on how much control I actually have, how much is within me, how I really write my own script and teach people how to treat me. I have certainly had a lot of growing pains but with each one I grew, and the moment I felt I was falling apart, I was actually falling into a more beautiful version of myself and a far better business woman, an unstoppable woman, if you will. Looking back, I actually appreciate it all so much more.

There is a saying, I don't know who came up with it, but it goes, "Something will grow from all this, and it will be you." I couldn't agree more with this sentiment, and I would have never known branching out on my own again back in 2015 would be such a whirlwind of growth personally, professionally and spiritually.

The following is some insight that I have learned along the way; owning a business can provide one with a great sense of accomplishment. It may sound rather simple at first, but the value of your business will depend on the value you are able to create. Many people believe they can get rich quick, start a business and become a millionaire overnight. This, I must say, is a HUGE misconception. We all see it, the Instagram entrepreneur online and their grand luxurious lifestyle, the ladies on Facebook with the kid on the hip of their perfect bodies and showroom homes, perfect nails etc. While traveling the world and running a business with her Giuseppe heels on, running after a toddler. Ha! If that's what you're expecting, good luck! It can be done, don't get me wrong. I too have kids, love to travel and have a killer heel collection but no one talks about the let downs, mascara running down your face in tears, and the days you want to go postal and runaway because, Heaven forbid, we don't appear "perfect". Side note sweetheart, most of these men and women I have found are full of crap that pretend to be so perfect. We call them, "broker jokers", in my industry and its usually the loudest guy in the room. Long story short, don't set yourself up for failure and don't let people intimidate you. They are not always what they appear to be, believe me. In my experience, you come to find that you have it going on a lot more than you think.

I am an investor and broker by trade, but I generally just refer to myself as a "great collaborator". *'I make it happen!!'* My companies are generalized as one, an investment advisory firm and the other a consulting firm. I work with Crypto currencies, various instruments and commodities, government tenders and trade. Most recently, some global government projects that are opening gateways to my true hearts passion; humanitarianism.

My partner in my advisory firm once asked me, in the beginning when we were brainstorming ideas and putting together our executive summaries etc, "Melissa, if you could do anything you want, what would it be? What would be your dream?" I knew without any doubts it would be Philanthropy. He too has the heart for such, hence why we put the name of Philanthropy in our company title, and you know what's funny? The universe really does give you what you want because all I have been working on, and the contacts I have made, have led me to such a place I can now more fully pursue that desire within me and make a great global impact.

Unstoppable woman, there is great power in what you put out there and in the words, titles and phrases you use. I named my companies very intentionally. The pyramid is energy and they can be found all over the world, I also knew I wanted to make an impact globally and boldly stated 'international' in my name when I only started because I knew what I wanted. So my advice is; be very intentional, build your dreams, your desires, your "lifestyle" for you and your loved ones. Oprah says it best when advising us to "create the highest, grandest vision possible for your life. Because you become what you believe." I am a firm believer in vision boards, I make a new one annually and am able to really reflect on everything I actually accomplished. It is such a gratifying practice! I encourage my children to do so as well.

It's not what you know but who you know, and it's not who YOU know but who knows you.

Networking

A highly important facet of any successful business. "Your network is your net-worth", a quote by Grant Cardone. Networking to me is one of, if not the most, essential part of your business because not only does it allow you to position yourself across varied markets, but it also helps diversify your strengths and mitigate your weaknesses by the power of leverage. What you may not be able to accommodate or provide, then there may be someone in your network that will.

Being recognized within your network as the go to and go getter, a person that can get things done, will help improve your value and, in the long run, drive your companies value and numbers. As we all know, word of mouth travels quickly and this would be the best form of advertising amongst your network, and thus, their extended networks. To bring success and be that unstoppable woman in business, ladies, we need to collaborate. Collaborating effectively and efficiently with others, and having good communication with your team and extended partners, opens more doors and effectively puts the term "work smarter, not harder" into action.

When it comes to doing business across borders, one must have patience and understanding of cultures to be able to communicate and meet the needs of the client. In my personal business, I find myself collaborating with multiple partners across the globe. I find that when collaborating with others it's important to keep in mind that each party has their own goals and objectives. It becomes an art form, if you will, to bring these goals and objectives into one key objective and goal, to create something each party will work towards. With the realization that the success of a given project will translate to the realization of the goals, objectives, dreams and desires of all involved.

Negotiation

Going into business, one MUST keep in mind that you will negotiate. I would suggest developing this skill early on as this is a key skill in business and in life. Pretty much in every aspect of life, we are constantly negotiating. Leveraging the power of negotiation, one can mitigate business risk, acquire and retain good clientele and further build value and growth. Business is not only about people but also a numbers game. One needs to work towards achieving the numbers through the mutually vested efforts of one's teams and clients. As a woman in business, I feel like this skill really needs to be fine-tuned. I'll be honest here, there will be times being a woman will come to your benefit, and in some cases, will be a disadvantage. We know there can be some special characters out there, however, this is where those good collaborations, a strong team and the perfecting of skills come in handy.

SELF-CARE, SELF-MOTIVATION AND MINDSET

Being self-motivated today seems harder than ever, with family and kids running around, it can be difficult to find the energy or motivation to pursue a business interest. It's important to develop a mind state that you will do what it takes to succeed.

Find your motivating factor, your WHY,
why do you do it?
What is it that drives you to want to be
successful in your business?

Mine is my children. I want to give them the absolute best of everything and I want to give them their mother. What kills me about that is since I've started having more and more success in my business, I've lost so much time. Working way more than I ever did in the corporate world. Working crazy hours because numerous clients are overseas, 7 days a week, 365 day a year. I remember I took a break for my birthday, which happens to be a holiday, and it was all of two days and people just about lost it. I began gaining weight from stress and never had time for me. I didn't have gym time or even time to enjoy a meal in peace or food prep like I wanted, or

7

really be in the moment with my children, the reason I was doing all of this in the first place. I started to resent my phone, and my kids did too.

I came to a crossroads of, 'geez, maybe this isn't worth it.?' I thought that at least if I worked for someone else, I could be left alone at some point. I would have hours and granted, sure, there was some networking events here and there, but it's not nightly. However, then I realized, 'No, if I do that, I am building someone else's dream', and that's not what I wanted to do.

I finally declared that my children deserved their mother to be in the present and not with the phone constantly attached to her ear. I finally declared that I deserved my own love and affection and expertise that I so willingly give others. Myself and my body, my temple the house of my soul, deserved to be well cared for. I decided to take control of my time and be in the moment and enjoy my life with my husband and children, to remember my WHY.

It's important to identify this and have laser focus towards your goal, to use your 'why' as your driving factor. Let this empower you and move you closer to your goals.

Relationships

Understanding interpersonal relationships and the creativity of one's clients, partners, employees, etc. Creatively drafting a plan of action, can help the business overcome or remove obstacles and barriers from entry into several business markets. With that being said, I feel like your relationships are literally everything!

I am in a people business and there's always a large element of trust that lies between parties, and for good reason. See, here is what I know and understand, although I am all about having the right lawyer/esquire and having iron clad contracts in place, let me tell you that at the end of the day, all a contract gets you is a court date. Court means time, and time is valuable. In fact, it's the most valuable thing we have, yet don't own. Now, will I let my lawyers take someone to court if they cross me? Absolutely! But do I want that time and negative energy used and in my realm? Absolutely not!

So, in an effort to avoid that, I chose who I work with very carefully.

I have had some hard lessons that taught me a lot. I came into business at a young age and was usually always the youngest girl in the room, if not the only girl in the room. At this stage, I am not always the youngest anymore and I am starting to meet more women in my industry that have become like sisters. We support each other and have each other's backs. I can honestly say that I have only had one catty experience in all my years, and that's says a lot for the great ladies in business. We clap for each other and lift each other up and celebrate one another's success, it's a beautiful thing. I hope this becomes a trend amongst women in all aspects.

Being in a male dominated industry (especially as I work on a global spectrum), I have really struggled to find the balance. Balance being that I want to keep my sweetness and nurturing nature, my femininity if you will, but I also don't want my kindness to be taken for weakness. Once upon a time, I was too trusting. I thought the golden rule applied in all facets, 'do unto others, as you want done unto you"; therefore, if I was of good moral and nature, others would reciprocate. In reality, I worked for a company that, one day, I came in and the CEO and his wife, who I was used to greeting daily, disappeared (like literally abandoned and left the state). Leaving the rest of us executives and higher-ups within the company to sort the pieces out. In my own business, I have had people I have trusted and brought to the table to meet other parties, to carry out their goals and visions. Only to be circumvented and told I couldn't be given details due to their own new non-disclosure agreements with the very parties I brought them to. I mean, talk about a slap in the face. That changed me. I was bitter for a moment, even more bitter when so many people don't make good on their word and leave you hanging with constant delay.

When you spend so much time and energy and not see the fruits of your labor, when you're made to look like a fool in front of your family etc. I came close to giving up, to walking away and then I remembered my 'why' again. I remembered what my friend/partner asked me when he said, "Melissa what is your dream?" I thought about a dear gentleman in my life that's building a dynamic movement that will change so many lives and is such a great man with a heart for God. So much so, that he calls God the CEO of his company and refers to himself as the Vice President.

I know this man and his vision and have seen his setbacks, his delays, the people who have tried to circumvent or down right steal his ideas, and yet he kept going and that's inspirational to me. Making my father, Daniel Lawrence, an altogether AMAZING man and businessman, proud. He passed away very unexpectedly within the beginning of my business success, but he was superman to me. So many referred to him as a living legend due to his larger than life personality, and I was very lucky to grow up with someone that taught me at a young age about having great faith. He always reminded me that I have to have the faith to move mountains and that I can do anything I set my mind to, due to the power that is in me. Now, how can I give up knowing that? How can I when I have a wonderful husband and five amazing children, four here on earth and one that I believe resides in Heaven and watches over his mama. I can't let them down and let all I have gone through in this life be in vain. See, I believe when we survive a lot in our life span, some of that is for us, but a lot of it, is for others. It gives us this empathy and this understanding that one can't quite grasp having not lived through certain things. I have also been blessed with some great relationships. My family friends and brothers in business that have my back, and I have theirs. Had I not chosen the path I did, I might not have met such great people. I may not have grown in the ways I have. If I didn't have the setbacks, I wouldn't appreciate the success as much.

If I didn't have the insecure men that wanted to dim my light and break me down to make them feel more like a "man," then I wouldn't appreciate the good people in my life. God has blessed me with men, that lift me up, have my back, and genuinely want me to be successful and shine. I genuinely attempt to always stay humble, respect others, keep my femininity, and no matter what, do not let my heart grow cold. I keep my fire and passion brewing inside of me because that passion is what makes me, ME, and makes me special and unique. Never lose your passion!

There are times, even most recently, when I am working on projects that can be somewhat intimidating regardless of my experience.

I am reminded what a dear pastor and friend, Kenneth Jackson Sr of Lighthouse Apostolic Ministries in Seattle, said to me. He hadn't seen me in a while and had no idea what I was going through or what I had been facing, but I asked him to pray for me prior to getting ready to take another trip overseas. Without hesitation, he looked me dead in the eye and said, "You are exactly where you are supposed to be. You are supposed to be sitting at that table, you belong at that table." That resonated with me so much, and assured me, giving me the confidence that whether I am meeting with a City Developer, a Prime Minister, President or Monarch of a country, a Minister, you name it; I am there because I am supposed to be. Either I am learning something, building something, breaking down barriers, or making it happen. As I mentioned earlier, I am there because I am supposed to be and I will strive to always give my absolute best in all I do.

In closing, my dear unstoppable woman of purpose, in business and in everything you do, you got this and you are exactly where you are supposed to be as well. Just remember to take good care of yourself every step of the way. Like the Buddha says, "You yourself, as much as anyone else in the entire universe, deserve your own love and affection". Never let anyone dim your shine or make you feel less than the goddess you are or cause you to second guess yourself when you are walking in your light and in your purpose. See, the enemy doesn't come as a stranger, but comes in the form of the ones closest to you, comes wrapped in love, or so it seems. Do not be discouraged, it means you are doing something right. Not everyone that starts with you on your journey will end with you, and that's okay. It doesn't make you un-loyal, it means that they were unworthy, or perhaps they served their purpose in your life or you in theirs. In all things, we grasp lessons. I love John Maxwell's way of putting things when he says, "We fail forward." See, we never really fail because, in all things, it's either a blessing or a lesson, and those lessons will level you up more than you can ever imagine.

You need those to progress. In a faith-based way of putting it; just like the spirit can't live in anything unclean, your walk, your journey, your success cannot be stifled in it either.

So have courage, don't be afraid to fail forward and know that there is nothing wrong with putting yourself first (I am still reminding myself of this daily). Remember how on the plane, a flight attendant reminds us to put our own mask on first before others? We can't be any good otherwise, both in an emergency and also in our daily walk. Why is it, as women, we have the hardest time with that?

Society can be unfair with its unrealistic expectations. I always feel like I am compromising something because, as women these days, we are doing more than ever. I am not saying don't shoot for being the most amazing woman you can be in every aspect, but what I am saying (and also reminding myself) is, cut yourself some slack. We are amazing. We really can have it all. Just don't compromise yourself in the process like I did. I hope my hard lessons will serve you well. My dear sister reading this, I applaud you every step of your journey. Remember, you can't ever beat the person that just never gives up, and also, remember to help someone else up too and appreciate those that have your back. We all need each other.

Now go be **Unstoppable!**

PART II

SARAH GRIFFITHS

"I didn't come this far to only come this far."

-Sarah Griffiths

SMASHING THE GLASS CEILING

BY SARAH GRIFFITHS

"I didn't come this far to only come this far."

-Sarah Griffiths

I t is interesting how our instinct is to keep ourselves small, to not blow our own trumpet and shout about our achievements! I love the title of this book "Unstoppable Woman in Business" but, until I got invited to co-author for it, I had not really thought about myself in that way. I do now though and have no idea why I did not recognise myself as that before. Why? Quite simply because; I have become and am an Unstoppable Woman in Business! I just didn't realise it before, all a part of keeping myself small, just doing my thing and not really thinking about how unusual, resilient, determined and tenacious I am to have achieved what I have.

How did I get here? Where is here? Where to next? The first two, I know the answer to and will share with you in this chapter. The last one is much harder to answer. I know where I have gone and I know where I want to go, but that is a picture of growth that evolves as I do. All three of my businesses are in the growth and development stage and have further to go, so here I say, watch this space.

For me, success is not just about running profitable businesses; the achievement is not necessarily the result. The income pays the bills but, like all businesses, there is no certainty of that and many outside factors can affect turnover, so the true benefit is in the journey.

Who have I become in the process? What have I learnt and how do I use that to now support others on their journey? Who will I become as the journey continues? It is all about the race, not the winning. I know that more than anything, I want to leave a legacy. Not a financial one necessarily, but a roadmap or a blueprint for doing life and business well. For acting with integrity at all times and being authentic. For being an outstanding employer.

Success for me happens when I come from a place of giving and my approach is, 'What can I give', not, 'What will I get'. It is a mantra that I have learnt. I apply it to life and to business, and I hope more than anything that my philosophy is apparent in this chapter as I encourage you to, "Leave everyone you encounter with an impression of increase"

All too often we look at people that we consider to be successful and we form an idea about them, "They must have had contacts, financial help, a great education, they obviously got lucky." Very recently someone told me that they looked at what I have achieved and assumed that my parents had money to help me. Well, nothing could be further from the truth.

Why do we do that? Make those judgements about people? Is it easier to think that because it explains why they have achieved more than we have? Funny that we don't automatically think, "They must have worked really hard, made sacrifices, taken risks, pushed themselves to the limit, really believed in themselves, had courage, set some extraordinary goals and been fearless and resilient." You have to be prepared to do ALL of the above to be successful in business. So, why don't we think about people in that way?

I currently run three businesses. I started in business seven years ago and I can tell you for a fact that NONE of the first descriptions apply to me, BUT all of the second do. I am just clearing this up early on so there are no misconceptions about me, or actually, about being in business in general. It is a really tough road to follow, if it was easy, everyone would do it! There is a reason they don't!

YOU ARE YOUR BIGGEST BARRIER TO SUCCESS

I already mentioned that I currently run three very diverse businesses so, how did that come about?

Any business, new or old, will have hurdles and barriers to success. It is easy to blame other people, external circumstances and situations, but the biggest barrier to my success was definitely myself. My husband also played a pivotal and very significant role in holding me back, operating from his own limiting beliefs around what I could and should be doing. That is the essence of my book "The Unlikely 7 Figure Entrepreneur."

Aside from the limits you place on yourself, you definitely need to be acutely aware of the role that others might play in holding you back from achieving your true potential. From the coaching and mentoring I now do, I understand that it does not matter what level of business someone is operating at; in general, we are our own worst enemies, and our self-doubt and mindset are our biggest barriers. We set ourselves a ceiling of what we expect from ourselves, what we think we can achieve and I can guarantee you that it is way too low! Let me assure you, specifically you! You are far more capable than you think you are but; you don't even need the negative input of other people to hold you back, you do a great job of that yourself. Others are literally just adding to what you have already placed in your own way.

Maybe, in just these few lines you can already relate to the point I am making here? I have got so much better at dealing with this now, I recognise those negative thoughts, words and beliefs for the safety instincts that they are. In the beginning, stepping way outside of a comfort zone, breaking your own glass ceiling for the first time, these self-imposed limits or feared beliefs are like pieces of elastic keeping you safe and reeling you back in when you try to take a step too far. You need to learn to ignore them if you are going to achieve anything at all. Recognising your self-doubt, lack of belief, or fears is in itself a big step to dealing with them. We are all different, but what remains the same is that we are all a product of our experiences and our environment. The environment we grew up in has a huge influence on who we are and how we see the world, ourselves and our role within the world. Even if we do not recognise or realise it, we have formed opinions and are operating to rules based on what happened around us when we were young. These then go on to affect us in our adult lives unless we recognise them as limiting and, reinvent new rules for ourselves.

For many, this will be the traditional story we are told, of what success looks like and we may have seen it modelled in our own families: go to school followed by university, get a 9-5 job in a steady, progressive career, have four-weeks of holidays a year, get that fabulous house with a huge mortgage, get married, have two kids and live happily ever after! Does that sound familiar? We just go along with the norm or what is expected of us without questioning it or exploring other avenues and modes of being. This is how people discover that they hate being a doctor, but became one because there has always been one in the family or their parents just expected it. Just recently I was talking to a woman who was distressed because her son did not want to go to university and she could not understand why; he was good at science and she wanted him to become a scientist. He wanted to do something physical around sports and she was really upset about this. Do you see how we get pressured to meet expectations and then find it hard to follow our own path?

Overcoming these expectations is one of the first barriers, rocking the boat, risking upsetting someone who wants/expects something else for you. It might take courage to just step out and be who you really are and follow your own dreams, make your own plans and create your own rules for life.

I shared these insights with you so you understand a bit about me and the business barriers I have overcome, and that my biggest barrier was myself and how I saw myself which was driven by very low self-esteem from being bullied about being poor when I was very young. Whilst it left me with extreme drive and a desire to succeed, I also did not see myself as good enough for the kind of environment I wanted to operate in and I constantly saw myself as a fraud waiting to be discovered as 'not good enough' and 'over reaching myself'. I also had a drive that was fuelled by my own core experience, "You have to work or you will be poor and your children will suffer", as this was my childhood experience and I applied it to my adult life. This was not necessarily a healthy place to be operating from as it made it very difficult for me to ever see my successes or to feel that I had achieved anything worthwhile. In my mind, I always came back to feeling not good enough and as if I should be doing more.

That is how I came to have not just one but, three businesses before I recognised my own worth and value. I have shared openly and honestly about how I was my own biggest barrier to life/business success and if this resonates with you, there are some key things you can ask yourself to help you move out of your own way. What do I want to do and why have I not done it yet? I suspect that you had an idea, something you wanted to do, so you told someone close to you who instinctively told you not to do it! Am I right? That would be our 40,000-year-old DNA and fear instinct kicking in to keep you safe. Before you share your hopes, dreams and plans with anyone, ask yourself this next question; what have they done and what do they know?

This tells you how QUALIFIED they are to actually give you helpful and relevant advice. You should also consider their motivations for any advice they give you. Even if it is subconsciously, people often have selfish reasons for directing you away from something you want to do. Maybe they want to keep you close or restrict your growth. Remember, your success makes others look ordinary! Who are you surrounded by? Make sure that you surround yourself with likeminded and positive people, the ones who support you and lift you up. Those who help you to believe in yourself and encourage you to be who you really are. Look at the people in your life, is there anyone you might need to cull? Maybe put some more distance between you or spend less time with them, or even no time at all?

Once you start to achieve more, sad as it is you need to understand that not everyone you know will be happy for you. You will lose some friends or find that people are saying negative things about you, if not to you. This will almost certainly happen, so be prepared for it. A negative person is VERY draining, don't allow them a place in your life where they can drag you down and suck the very life and soul out of you. If you have anyone like that in your life, well, there goes your hopes and dreams! They will crush, limit and restrict you, to keep you at their level.

What help do I need and from whom?

Don't make the mistake of thinking that you have to be, know and do everything. You have a gift and a genius zone, stick to it and get the help you need with all of the other tasks that are not in your expert field. Get an expert to do them and direct your talents in the right direction. If you try to be/do everything, you will end up burnt out, disillusioned and will not be doing your business any favours at all. If you can take on board what I have shared so far, you will be travelling in the right direction to moving out of your own way and creating the business of your dreams. Work with a coach!

Personally, I have several at any time, for the different aspects of my life or business that I need support with and, I suggest you do the same. Not only will the right coach challenge and support you but, they will help you create strategies to support what you say you want to achieve. When you come up against hurdles, which you will, they will get you over them and into your next growth phases. The majority of very successful people have a coach, a mentor or a team so, why wouldn't you? No man is an island or self-made, we all need the right support from the right people to achieve our true potential.

BE A TRUE LEADER

My first business, which I started seven years ago in March of 2011, was a franchise in hospitality with 'The Coffee Club', Australia's largest franchise café brand. It was a great place to start and has served me well as a business learning ground. It was similar to having a business coach in that; I recognised that whilst I wanted to run a café or restaurant, I did not actually know anything about it. In the previous section I mentioned getting help from those who know better than you do, well, franchising is exactly that, on a very large scale.

For me it was a great place to start because they taught me everything I needed to know about running a successful café- about processes, ordering, finances, etc. BUT the biggest piece of the puzzle was me and I quickly realised that whilst I might be the owner, I was definitely not a leader. I just did not have the necessary people and leadership skills (as I saw it) to competently lead a team. My key skills were in customer service due to my years in sales, but I was woefully unprepared and unable to handle a team of people. One of my biggest issues was my own lack of self-belief and low self-esteem which lead me to immediately feel inadequate amongst some of my employees, as they had experience in hospitality and I did not.

What that did initially was, to give me some big challenges, (which I will cover here) that I was not personally equipped to deal with and it definitely highlighted to me where my shortcomings were. Just like me, of you are in this situation, you have a choice: Ignore, hope for the best and stick your head in the sand or, the best option; challenge yourself to become better in those areas! Get the help, support and training you need to become unstoppable.

Rather than ignore my shortcomings, one of the huge benefits was that I recognised my barriers and have spent the last seven years learning how to be a LEADER rather than just a business owner. There is a big difference between those two, so please take this on board. Needless to say, I no longer have low self-esteem or issues managing my teams! In fact, I think I have developed into a very competent leader that people want to work with. I am not perfect and am constantly working on improving who I am and what I bring to my businesses, especially in how I support and manage my staff. Leading with emotional intelligence has become my passion. I expect it of myself and ALL of my managers and supervisors. My initial problems with managing a team were varied, but I learnt a lot from them and now help other business owners facing similar issues.

The industry and situation are irrelevant, being a leader is about understanding and being equipped to deal with people in some-times awkward and complicated situations. I wonder if you can relate to any of the following, which were my main shortcomings that I addressed to become the business leader that I am today.

MY LACK OF EXPERIENCE

When I first opened my Coffee Club, I was very grateful to the team that were hired as many of them had hospitality experience so it was easy for them to learn their roles. There was a downside to this though, it was also easy for them to make me feel very insecure! As if I did not know what I was doing when they constantly questioned my decisions and made changes, undermining my authority. I placed way too much trust in them too, as I often felt that they knew what they were doing and I did not.

This was apparent in various ways but especially in the following:

- *Working more than their rostered hours and telling me I had not given them enough time to complete tasks and they needed longer. This meant they got paid more.*
- *Generally gossiping about me and undermining any authority and any respect I might have had.*
- *Constantly complaining about staff that I employed and decisions I made.*

- *Openly telling me I did not know what I was doing and changing things that I put in place.*

Then two senior staff started a relationship which became acrimonious and adversely affected everyone. The business was not doing well and had got to the point where I did not want to be there. I was way out of my depth, being manipulated and controlled by my staff who had no respect for me at all, I had no idea what to do and then fate leant a hand and everything changed. The manager who should have been my biggest support, but who was totally undermining me, suddenly left, phew! In that moment, I decided to learn to be the manager and leader that I needed to be, and that I was going to do what I should have done a long time ago, manage the business and the staff myself without the support of a supposedly experienced manager. I had previously been too intimidated by the experienced team members to do this, but now, I was determined. In fact, I knew that if I was to turn the business around then I had to step up and make some sweeping changes. That had to start with me, how I was showing up and how the staff saw me. I was definitely not perfect, but it was the start of me growing into a leader instead of an owner and my business to start thriving.

Clearly there was some resistance to this and some staff left, but that left me with a core group of staff who I wanted to work with, who had wanted things to change and were now looking forward to working with me. One of those, my current manager, is still with me and other staff members have been with me for three to five years. So, how did I turn it around, and what were the key lessons?

YOUR PEOPLE ARE YOUR POWER

I personally worked really hard to gain the respect of my team. I mean physically hard, on the floor, in the kitchen, at the till, coffee machine, everywhere. It became really important to me to understand every role and aspect of my business because then I COULD SET THE STANDARD. Far from not understanding my business, I spent the next 12 months mastering every key role so I was one of the few who could manage in every position.

Not only did this give me the confidence that I needed, BUT I could see where the problems were and work out how to solve them. I could see where standards could be improved, who was good at their job and who was not. Far from being intimidated, I became supremely confident in my ability. I worked alongside them and created an environment where they worked with me and not for me. I started to understand everyone's strengths and weaknesses, and very importantly for me, what was important to them in the workplace. I had created a very happy workplace and I wanted to keep it that way.

I started to look for ways to foster staff loyalty; I felt that if I could give them more than they would usually get from a job in hospitality, in return I would also get more from them. This was very important for my ethos of excellence. I did not just want another café, I wanted an exceptional one where the customer experience is over and above what they were expecting. Now, how was I to motivate my staff to provide that standard and also share that vision?

As mothers with young children, mortgages, school fees and car payments there were several things they wanted, not usually found within hospitality, and it really came down to:

- *Security*
- *A fixed income, i.e. a salary instead of casual hours*
- *Fixed hours so they could plan*
- *All of this close to home so they could also manage their other commitments*

- *Variety, not to be stuck in one role*
- *Opportunities to learn new skills*

So, in the interests of stability and reliability and against the usual conditions of employment within hospitality, I gave them what they wanted and it was the best thing I ever did. All of my full-time staff are salaried rather than casual, and even my casual staff have extensive training and opportunities to become competent in a variety of skills. I now have a long standing, happy and loyal team, all totally on board with my vision and expectation as far as standards go. Our staff turnover is minimal which our customers love. Our team is skilled and passionate about what they do and they are as invested in the business's success as I am.

It was this attitude and this move, as well as generating this kind of relationship with my staff, that lead me to then, four years ago in April of 2014, leave my Coffee Club in the capable hands of a committed and diligent team and open a second restaurant 300 kms away. Not a franchise this time but an evening fine dining restaurant that was in decline and I wanted the opportunity to apply what I now knew about running a hospitality establishment and turn it around.

BE UNSTOPPABLE AND CHASE YOUR DREAM

So, over a period of three years I had totally transformed myself as a person, a business owner and leader. From someone who was scared of doing the wrong thing and thought very little of herself to someone who now had the drive and confidence to open a second, independent restaurant. Not just a new business, but a totally different type of eating and dining venue requiring a whole new approach and a different set of skills.

As a couple, we now had a lot of money invested in two businesses. It was literally all of our equity and every cent we could borrow, not just from banks but from family too. Yes, it was a scary time, especially as hospitality is very unpredictable! People ask me, "How did you know it would work?" Well, we didn't. Sometimes in life you just have to be brave, take huge risks (calculated ones, not foolish ones) and step way out of your comfort zone to achieve something extraordinary. The reward and return on my investment have been incredible, although, at times the work load has seemed impossible.

To grow a business in this way you not only have to be very determined, tenacious and definitely not afraid of a lot of hard work, but there is one key thing you really do have to embrace that many people struggle with and that is *delegation*. With two businesses 300km apart, obviously I could not work in both of them all of the time, and here is where my experience and growth running the 'Coffee Club' really became beneficial. I had a full working knowledge of the business I was placing under management, so I understood the various issues as they arose and was able to assist in solving them, without taking responsibility from those in charge. I could input enough to help but still leave them in charge and responsible for resolution.

I had set the standards and had a loyal team to support me which meant that I could step away and be as certain as I could be that the team, led by the manager, would work to the same standards whether I was there or not. I had great confidence that, that would be the case. Now, four years later, it remains the foundation that underpins both of my restaurants as the management and staff at both follow my lead and work to incredibly high standards.

If you want to grow your business, lead from the top and set an exemplary standard for your staff to follow. What happened from there was completely unexpected and lead to my third business which I had not actually planned at all.

UNEXPECTEDLY UNSTOPPABLE!

I found that for various reasons people started to come to me for advice about different aspects of how to do life! It seemed that whilst I just took it in my stride, people were fascinated by what I or rather we were doing. I say we because I could not do it without the support of my husband. He has his own job but, still assists me outside of hours and weekends. People approached me for advice on many different aspects of what I was doing: how to manage two businesses so far apart, how to ensure the standards were maintained, how to set those standards in the first place, how we managed our relationship over that distance, how did we juggle such busy lives, and how had we been married for so long? People who knew just seemed to be fascinated by what we were achieving.

I found that people were looking to me as an example and for mentorship, and I really enjoyed being able to help and support them in various aspects of their lives based on my own experience. I started coaching without looking for that avenue and was just thrilled by being able to support and encourage people to step up, step out and go for their dreams and that is how the third business sallyg.com began.

I decided that what I should do is use my experience and everything I knew and had learnt, to coach other people who were struggling to achieve or even visualise their own true potential. Because of my own challenges and the limiting beliefs about myself that I had overcome it seemed a natural niche for me as, whatever someone thinks their problem is it invariably comes down to those limiting beliefs and that self-imposed glass ceiling. Yes, there are other factors to consider but, nothing can be achieved until those self-sabotaging stories are dealt with once and for all! So, I help people recognise and overcome those first and then we can work on business start-up and growth. You need to understand that to do more, you need to become the person who can!

So, faced with a demand for what I had to offer, I decided to properly launch my third business! Which was the catalyst for another intense journey of discovery and learning for me. based on my own experiences, how I had thought about myself and what I had overcome, I realised that if I was to really help people become the best possible versions of themselves I needed to know a whole lot more! I wanted to understand the neuro science and workings of the mind and what drives us to stick with the familiar? What keeps us stuck etc.

I really got out of my own comfort zone and indulged in endless hours of research and study to discover the science behind why we are, who we are. To be honest, it was fascinating! And learning and study became my new hobby! I also selected and worked with my own mentors and coaches to learn as much as possible about the process of taking someone from where they are to where they want to be and that, included myself! I was developing and growing as a person and a leader and business owner at a very rapid rate. I also had a whole new area of business to learn.

I realised that I wanted to reach as many people as possible, and that meant learning the very complex and confusing business of online courses, marketing and membership sites. I was already running two businesses and Marc, my husband, had his own very demanding corporate position taking up at least 50 hours a week. There was also the logistics of the distance between the two businesses and the amount of travel involved. It really was a very intense 18 months and I do not think either of us has ever learnt so much in such a short space of time, or faced so many difficult challenges.

If you are looking at your next step, wondering how you can possibly make it happen, then I hope that our journey inspires you!

Yes, there were many, many times when I was totally exhausted, feeling out of my depth and thinking, "What have I done?", but I knew, beyond any doubt that I had uncovered my true passion and purpose. Every time I mentored or coached someone, I was rewarded with knowing that I had a positive impact on their life and all they wanted to be and do. So, that and all of the positive feedback kept me going. All I can say is, it has been an unexpected and incredible journey. I have no doubt that as I continue to serve and support others ALL of my businesses will reap the rewards as I expand who I am and my vision for my life. It has been a hard road but, there is nothing to match the sheer pleasure and joy of touching people's lives in a positive way.

I have discovered the freedom of self-actualisation! To see myself as limitless, rather than limited and to help others see themselves that way too! I continue to extensively invest in myself, my own personal growth and my commitment to my businesses. To my staff and everyone who knows or meets me, my intention is always to be a positive influence, a calming but challenging presence and to leave everyone I encounter with an impression of increase.

I sincerely hope that my story and experience will inspire you and encourage you to either start in business, or to grow in yourself and reach further than you thought was possible. Look outside of the obvious and expected for opportunities. Trust and believe in yourself, and most importantly, ask for the help you need when you need it.

Please, reach out to me if you would like me to help you become 'Unstoppable' or to just get started.

Here's to the unstoppable you!

PART III

VERONIKA WHYTE

"We forget to remind ourselves that overnight success is often decades of work and personal self-mastery behind the scenes."

-Veronika Whyte

SUCCESS BEYOND LIMITS

BY VERONIKA WHYTE

"We forget to remind ourselves that overnight success is often decades of work and personal self-mastery behind the scenes."

-Veronika Whyte

It was an early spring in Russia, the first of April 2008, some patches of the snow were still on the pavements, and it was about zero degrees at night. "I'll just grab my coat, I'll be right back", I said to my friend and rushed upstairs to my studio apartment on the second floor. It was the end of a working day and I was looking forward to sharing dinner with my friends, to have a great time together, they had prepared a few jokes and tricks to laugh about on Fool's Day. What happened next, we often call the moment that changed the course of events in life or the defining moment. No matter how you name it, I wasn't prepared for what I saw. Well, first of all, I could see nothing. It was dark, pitch black, in front of the door of my apartment. I thought something happened with the electricity and the power went off, I couldn't see a thing. A moment later I sensed something was not right, I couldn't name it but my stomach squeezed and twisted for no apparent reason. Then it registered, it was a smell, chocking and tickling the nose, the smell I will never forget, the smell of ashes. What I started to realise wasn't sinking in my mind, all I thought was, 'This can't be happening, how so, not to me?!'

I pushed the door, went down the hall and saw a bunch of neighbours gathered together with lit up candles in their hands. "Veronika!", they exclaimed with worried faces, somebody was weeping. "What the hell is going on here?", I yelled at them. Still not quite grasping the concept that it was not just a mean joke, I turned around to the doorway where my door used to be just before I left to work. I stepped into the darkness and looked at the window, which was shattered into pieces; the window I loved to look through in the morning, where I could see a beautiful tall tree outside. Cold wind blew in and brought a stronger wave of burnt-down-to-ashes-apartment smell to my nose. The glass screeched under my feet as I stumbled upon the things on the floor, still not being able to see what they were. The people behind me shed the light for me so I could see. I looked at them saying nothing as they mumbled something like, "it just started, they're not sure how." I pulled out my phone from my pocket and called my friend, "I think we need to cancel our dinner, could you come upstairs? There was a fire in my apartment." "Nice try, Veronika," she chuckled, "It's a Fool's Day. I'm not a fool to follow that joke, it's not funny anyway." I could barely squeeze a smile, "I have no idea what to do, please come", and I hung up.

Half an hour later I spoke with the neighbours, who didn't know much. Apparently, it had just happened two hours earlier and they were scared about what they were going to do now when all their possessions were gone within moments. I called my mum and sister to let them know what happened, and to reassure them that I was okay. I told them I wasn't at home at the time and that the cause of the fire would be identified later by the police, who were coming in the morning. I did everything with no panic, no emotions, no particular thoughts. My friend was still there, I turned to her and said, "Let's go, I can't stay here any longer, we will come back in the morning." She then drove me to her place, and on the way there, I sank into the seat. All of a sudden, I felt exhausted and my eyes started swelling with tears. First hot and stingy drops fell on my hands, I cried silently, I couldn't stop. The tears gushed from my eyes and streamed down, I sobbed inconsolably. I was terrified, I couldn't comprehend what I had done wrong that this would happen to me. What was I supposed to do now, where would I live, how was I going to face the next day? How was I going to find strength and the money to get by and start all over again? I remembered how hard I'd worked for this apartment to come true for me. How I saved every penny, how happy I was to move in one year earlier, how proud I was of my achievement to own my first place at the young age of twenty-four. I had finally completed the renovation and decoration of this tiny place, which I called mine. I was happy to be able to live independently, to come home after work and chillax in my own universe. Now it was gone.

We went upstairs to my friend's place, I sat with her in the kitchen, not able to move, too overwhelmed with thoughts and emotions. She poured me a drink, something very strong like whiskey. I never had a shot of spirits before, but I was in such low spirits, I figured some extra help would be appropriate. Then I had another one and another one. A few minutes later, I was asleep on the couch.

If you allow me, my dear unstoppable visionary, to let me introduce myself before I proceed with the story. My name is Veronika, it is 2018 now, and at the time of the fire I was a young lady of twenty-five, an aspiring teacher of cultural linguistics and literature with an entrepreneurial touch, running my own private teaching centre.

I was born in Russia, the city of Ufa, one of the five largest cities in the country. It is the most spacious of towns with the population of over two million, located on the shores of a beautiful river called Belaya (translated as 'white'). I grew up in a family of four; my mum, dad, younger sister and myself. My family was a 'normal' family with very busy, young parents in their early twenties who tried to make a living for their two girls and provide the best they could. Although I love my parents dearly, as a child I had longed to spend more time with them. Four years senior, I had grown up early to help my mum look after my little sister so that she could do her chores after work while my father was still finishing his engineering degree at the university.

During those years I found my consolation in books, in their characters stories, descriptions of emotions, lives, thoughts, details. It was as if I could step into their world, see their very core, and see them for who they really were. Reading fast and a lot had helped me to become one of the brightest pupils at school. I had an amazing teacher who saw my eagerness to learn and somehow convinced the teaching committee that I could skip a whole year of studies by taking the exams only. So, when I skipped grade two jumping from grade one to three, I liked it and repeated it three times. It allowed me to complete school three years earlier than my peers. With some zig zags on the way, I received a scholarship for university and embarked on my studying journey. Why do I share all of this? Sometimes in our life circumstances, which can seem unfortunate at first sight, turn into our personal gifts. I dare to say, all greatness in every single individual comes from the challenges and struggles that they overcame. In fact, I haven't met a single person who has achieved personal success and hasn't faced the darkest of times then rose like a Phoenix from those ashes. My curiosity about people's spirit and authentic stories made me passionate about knowledge, education, and most importantly, sharing their message; which has created the foundation for my business success later in life.

You see, there are situations and phases in life that build us when we look for the answers, when we need someone's support. We might admire other people and strive to be like them, yet often they deem unachievable. We forget to remind ourselves that overnight success is often decades of work and personal self-mastery that happens behind the scenes. We see people shine in their glory and that is beautiful; however, when we are not yet there, we dream and desire to become unstoppable on a mission with purpose trying to fulfil our vision, looking around for the clues. We might not have a person around us to model excellence at that very moment or we cannot gain access to them, but we could always read a book. We could enter someone's world via the story that preceded the success. While reading we could be understood, listened to, nurtured, reassured and inspired; we can connect with our inner resources of possibilities.

I learnt to read at the early age of four, and at five I started going to the local library where everyone knew my mum and looked after her little daughter. Stepping into writing myself and co-authoring three books so far was not by accident, clearly books are part of who I am. I love to be inspired by other people and would also like to inspire others through my experiences and interpretation of knowledge. Hopefully it will provide the insight for you to become an unstoppable visionary of purpose. During the moments of doubts, uncertainty, and questioning myself on who am I to dream big, the wonderful heroes of the stories were demonstrating to me that they were just like me once upon time. They felt the same burning ambition inside them, they achieved things in life but the sense that there was something beyond them was whispering in their ear at night. They would day dream and look for guidance, until one day, it would click within them as if it had always been there from the beginning. They realised that you need to let your guard down and open the locked up inner resources which are hidden in our hearts; the rawness, the authenticity.

So, I graduated and was lecturing at the university at the age of twenty-two, which made me one of the youngest on the faculty. Although I loved the novelty of teaching and was deeply engaged and committed to delivering the best value I could, I soon realised I could not build enough income for the lifestyle I dreamt of with only having the job I had. I was paid a fixed amount at an hourly rate and there was no way to leverage off that. The same books I read revealed to me that there are wonderful places in the world, various cultures, picturesque landscapes, and I wanted to experience all of it. Travelling in style needed, well, money. Remember me? I always looked for the clues, and I did what I could do the best at – learning the strategies of building extra income. I looked around myself for a role model and my mum was a perfect match. Although she had no desire to read any books in her life, she had an amazing talent of creating business opportunities wherever she went, she was the light of any party and she knew so many people, her address book couldn't fit any more. She had that natural ability to care for people and build strong relationships with them, which I established later on. Afterwards, when I was studying business and marketing, I could put the name on what my mum was great at; namely, it was building rapport, branding and networking. I admired my mum and decided to model someone who had the results in business, so there I was, registering my own teaching business. In a short few months I found myself booked-out by building relationships with wonderful students and providing outstanding value. I started travelling and saving for my apartment. I didn't own a car, deciding it was not a priority for me and used public transport instead. For me, this was a necessary sacrifice at the time. I often found that people who aim for perfect balance in life are simply not ready to temporarily substitute comfort for long-term success.

At the age of twenty-four, I signed the contract of purchase for my apartment and moved in. It was a tiny place in the middle of the city, rather crowded, and I could hear my neighbours behind my walls but, boy, I was feeling happy, independent and on top of the world. No more renting, and way more travelling. That year I travelled to Australia during the holidays for the very first time and promised myself to go back, a little longer the next visit, in order to have sufficient time on my hands to explore the diverse parts of that beautiful place. Once my vacation was over, I went back to work. My business was giving me a great amount of satisfaction, and my students were providing our school with positive feedback and referred new people. I felt great and in control of my own destiny, feeling even better by planning my epic birthday party on the ninth of April. All that changed over one night on Fool's day, a week shy from the planned celebration.

The morning after the fire came, I didn't feel great and wished that the first hangover headache was the only worst thing that had happened to me. Here I was, a person with no place to live, no clothes to wear, no documents to identify myself, no photographs to look at. I wore a light dress and had only my favourite handbag, my laptop, a phone and a necklace of uncertainty. I called into the school and headed off to the place of the fire where I needed to provide the police with some information. In the light, the burnt down place looked cold and abandoned. I saw the object I stumbled upon the night before, it was my new pair of designer boots. Opening my wardrobe, my mink coat looked sad and wet from the fire-fighters' water and foam, I noted in my head that I should have worn it that morning. Next, I saw my pearls in the ashes. I dug them out with a pencil I found on the floor and put them in a plastic bag. My bookshelf was burnt on the outside but a bit of cash was safe behind the books; unfortunately, my documents were in the front drawer and were completely burnt, including my passport and certificates of degrees.

I was picking up the partially burnt photographs, sending some papers to fly out of the window. I felt exposed and vulnerable to the world, everyone could see me, they could see every part of my life, I couldn't stop it. Looking around, my bright home yesterday seemed far away, part of my life simply burnt down. To say that a month after the fire was tough, does not even describe it. I needed to fix the apartment by inserting new windows and contacting special cleaning services, because, let me tell you, nothing can clean off the smell of burnt ashes. I tried to restore my degree certificate with the average mark of 95%, but there were some problems with the originality of the document. Ten years ago, not everything was stored electronically yet. It was the time of transformation and conversion to the proper backing up of data, digital archives and so on. My home insurance didn't cover anything because that was the last thing I had cared about when I was excitedly buying my very first place to live. My business depended a 115% on my presence, so I had to continue on as if nothing had happened, doing all the work in the background.

Did I learn some lessons? Yes, I did. It taught me about vulnerability, it taught me necessary safety measures I needed to have in place, even if they are all only strategies to implement. I learnt the power of resourcefulness, the power of standing through the wind of change as it smashes into your face, the power of going through the dark tunnels and remembering everything I learnt from people who were in challenging situations before me. My biggest lesson of all, the one I promised to myself, was that I would never back down on my values, I would never give up on me, on my dreams and on sharing my message. I am not about helping people, although, I believe there is a bit of arrogance in that. I am about showing people the possible way, demonstrating to them that they are not alone and that no matter what, they can handle it. If it was easy, everyone would be successful. Success requires strength, consistency, vulnerability, courage and readiness to start everything from the beginning again.

This disaster led me to sharing the art of conscious business with business owners by having a structured security cushion. Not the addiction to safety, that is another extreme, but the structured management of force-major circumstances. Benjamin Disraeli once said, "Hope for the best but be prepared for the worst". Based on my personal experience of being in various business activities for over fifteen years now, equipped by certificates in business, marketing and financial services, I will share below some practical guides on what has to be taken into consideration so that you can have a piece of mind. If anything happens, you will look straight into your eyes and confidently say to yourself, "I can handle this".

Losing everything you own changes your perspective on things, of course it would. You will experience your version of loss or letting go, along with your version of feeling and owning the experience of becoming an unstoppable visionary. Someone who doesn't halt because of the hurdles, but instead moves forward because of them. These people understand that there are no great achievements without sacrifice, doing the work and constantly uncovering new resources within our self. That month after the fire when I borrowed the money to renovate my studio, to buy new furniture, clothing and other lifestyle things. I decided to be in control of my finances on another level instead of wishing and hoping that it would work out itself. It isn't enough to wish and wait for a better system or a better time when you have less on your hands, you must decide to drive your own vehicle of a fulfilled life.

Nobody has total control over sudden or unexpected events, but you do have control of being prepared to continue your mission, to sustain your business, and to look after yourself, your family and the people you work with. If you think money doesn't buy you happiness, you are right, but it can definitely give us choices. Not everyone wants more choices, but if you do want them, the one way to have these choices is to have the finances to act on them. Wealth is a decision, success in business, is a decision. You can do it, you have your unique story and your individual circumstances, but you are not the exception. Model excellence, share your results, build the strategies and above all, invest in your personal mastery because if you ever face the challenge of losing everything and there is a high probability of it, you can always start over, rebuild yourself, and your material assets. The most valuable and precious asset is in your mind and heart. This is where the gold is stored, where you can always access it, melt it into different shapes and forms, and create a new reality you choose.

I established my current consultancy business, "Success Beyond Limits", five years ago, ironically on the first of April, and I used the success principles again and again. It provides me not just with financial security, but it allows me to ride the roller coaster of unexpected situations in my everyday business routine. It gives me resilience, the sense of certainty that I will be able to handle the uncertainty and adventure, which is rather a common denominator in many business transactions. Being successful in business, for me, is providing phenomenal value to people I work with, for people who trust me, creating transformation and outstanding results. To see people's dreams come true, to observe them discovering who they are and what is possible for them, to be part of the process of metamorphosis from cocoon to chrysalis, to see their wings growing and finally flying freely and sharing their unique beauty.

Each individual is a universe. Each and every one sees the world differently in their mind's eye. I believe it is important to continually think about the sort of universe you want to live in and how you are going to create it. In order to implement 'how', for example the steps to your financial freedom or success in business, the most important part of the process is defining your why and upgrading your mindset. From a business perspective, creating your universe is about claiming your uniqueness by applying your personality, vision and creativity. These characteristics are uniquely yours, and by implementing them into your business brand, you will create a value that no one has encountered before. As a business owner you must be a leader, and a leader has a particular set of skills and personality mix which creates the energy that inspires other people to follow their vision.

Being the best version of yourself is a dynamic process, not a static event. You must continually look for the opportunities to enhance your abilities, never lose the desire to extend yourself. The more setbacks you experience, the more you will surprise yourself at what you are capable of. In fact, setbacks in business are the indicators that you are moving forward and progressing. Stick to your vision and values because people want to be able to rely on you, the only surprise you want to present people with is your ability to exceed their expectations.

In the end, I would love to say that dreaming big is great, but remember that a big life, the life on your terms when you live your passion and inspire others, comes greater responsibility. It doesn't come easy on a social media plateau. It requires consistent effort, willingness to push through your limits, to grow, to face the wind of challenge and hail of necessary actions. It also requires the ability to enjoy the sunshine and freshness of the air after rain. Make every mistake, setback and challenge count. Force yourself to laugh in the toughest of times. You must learn to be happy where you are now.

If you can't enjoy where you are, there is no achievement that will help you to feel better tomorrow. You absolutely must choose to be grateful for your current circumstances, both positive and negative.

Yes, at the time of the event, there might be a period of anger, disappointment, grief, deep sadness. Do not resist it, go with it and meet your new self on the other side. You will emerge from the darkest waters to the surface where you will see the new horizons of an infinite sky. Remember the Lotus, one of the most beautiful flowers of wisdom, grows from murky water. It does not matter where you start, it matters where you are heading, where your intentions soar.

Yes, hiking and climbing the mountain towards your goals might be a daunting journey. Some summits take time to reach. Staying true to who you are is not an easy task. Figuring out who you are is even harder. Life is about growth – exposing yourself to various experiences, it is the only way to learn about yourself.

Always remember, my dear Unstoppable Visionary of Purpose, you will ultimately reach your goals if they mean enough to you. Give yourself permission to claim your power, to pursue your journey. This is the only permission you need. If not you, then who, and if not now, then when? Create the reality for your dreams to be fulfilled, the legacy to be proud of. Enjoy the process, and be prepared to experience the miracle of being authentically you. I, my dear visionary, look forward to celebrating your success together!

PART IV

HAZEL TODD

"Never let the lack of something stand in your way, if you can't find what you are looking for, be true to your feminine self and create it."

-Hazel Todd

THE UNSTOPPABLE SILVER LINING

BY HAZEL TODD

"Never let the lack of something stand in your way, if you can't find what you are looking for, be true to your feminine self and create it."

-Hazel Todd

I come from a family of entrepreneurs. My father, and my eldest brother both left school at the age of fifteen. In today's maddening world, where multiple degrees are somehow equated to success, it would seem that the odds were stacked against them. But the one thing that cannot be taught at school is entrepreneurialism, or the desire to be in business for yourself, to forge your own way and be the captain of your own vessel.

I was born in England. At the time, my father worked for British Railways and my mother stayed at home. Wanting a better life for us, when I was at the age of four, we moved to Africa. I'll be frank with you and say that I do not really understand the reason why we moved to what was called Rhodesia at the time. It was in the grips of a civil war, but it was a different life for us, even though my father still worked for the railways. I think though, that my father was still in search of something more, but the responsibility of a wife and three children meant he could not make any rash decisions. Soon enough, however, he found new work in the office equipment industry.

Then one day, things changed. My father was fired from his job, just like that, and for no apparent reason. We were devastated and in fear of what might happen. While the civil war was over, times were still very tough in what was by then, Zimbabwe. Mass shortages of even the most basic of items; milk, bread, petrol and a bunch of other things I was probably unaware of at the time, already meant we were doing without. As children we accept so much of the way things are. This was not the time or place to be entrepreneurial, and in hindsight, it made no sense to invest in a country where we were essentially no longer welcome in due to the change in government. Any money that you did have could not be taken out of the country, there was no safety net.

I remember the concern on my father's face as we became aware of what had happened. He had always protected his family, and showed very little of what he was feeling or the true depths of his concerns, but my brothers and I knew better than to partake in the conversation of the future direction that our lives would take. I suppose we simply trusted that he would ensure that it would all work out, and that he would do as he had always done and take care of us.

Suddenly, things all changed again, and if my memory serves me well enough, probably the very next day. You see, the man who had fired my dad offered to go into business with him, to set up a business in the neighbouring country of Botswana. It would probably have only been the second such office equipment business in the capital city of Gaborone at the time. While Botswana was less developed than Zimbabwe in those days, it did not suffer the same political upheaval that Zimbabwe was going through. Botswana was in peace and had enormous growth potential with its export of diamonds and beef to Europe. In fact, Botswana was one of the few countries in Africa that transitioned peacefully from a colonial to an independent state, and was one of the most rapidly growing economies too.

So, as things would turn out, my father losing his job was probably one of the best things that could have happened to us. My father's business, and then multiple businesses, went from strength to strength, with the man who had fired him a few years ago, eventually being bought out of that first business that started it all. My father was his own boss, and we were so very proud and in awe of him. He worked hard, he was sensible in all his dealings, and he wasn't in it to be what he termed a '*brylcreem boy*', all coiffed up and on show, trying to make a good impression. He was understated in his success, simply going to work every day and doing what needed to be done.

This was nothing that was taught at school, but my two brothers and I each learnt something very valuable, and we each came to run our own businesses. Now while it might seem that I am bashing education, not so. I value education highly, as did my father, who encouraged me to go to university and find a profession. Indeed, I was the first in my family to ever attend university.

So, I graduated university with a Bachelor of Commerce, then went onto law school in South Africa. After law school I returned home to Botswana to start my career and family with a two-year contract as a junior lawyer. While my only real understanding of working life had been a few part time jobs here and there, pursuing one's career after investing years on education was quite another experience.

After two years on the job, working for another, it was very clear that this was not the path for me. At the end of my two-year contract at that law firm, I was becoming the top fee earner in the firm, and the only female lawyer. The men, however, were receiving perks that I was not receiving, and that was not okay with me. It should never be okay with anyone.

I handed in my notice and rented a small office space that also offered some secretarial services and hung out my shingle, with several of my client's following me to my new practice. I still have that brass wall plaque to this day. It was then that my *first* business, 'Hazel Todd Attorneys, Notaries and Conveyancers', was born.

The one thing that I think greatly helped me get through those first few years of business was in keeping my expenses down. I have seen many businesses opt for the glitzy offices and a workplace full of people, who may have very little to do. All show and little substance. But I think sub-consciously I was taking a leaf out of my father's business book, and sticking to what was important, with the long-term goal always in mind for my business to thrive.

On this I would say, do what you feel is right for you and your business, not what others expect of you. Steer clear of the temptation for appearances over results. Your clients only want to know that you can help them, that you will take care of their pain points. So, consider how you can give your business the best chance to grow and last through the learning process, rather than simply working for your landlord's benefit.

Let technology be your friend. Automate and set up your processes in the beginning, so that you can efficiently produce the work. Always continue to refine and learn. Running a business is a learning and growth process. Your market will change and businesses that thrive know how to adapt.

In 2005, my husband at the time and I decided that moving to Australia would give our children greater opportunities. We sold our businesses and our property in Botswana, packed up all our worldly possessions into a container, and made the move to Melbourne.

If you were to ask yourself the question of who and what you are, you would no doubt define yourself in a number of ways; wife, mother, business owner and so on. One of the ways I defined myself was as a lawyer. That was who I was. When we arrived in Australia, I was no longer a lawyer, I was not qualified to practice law. I found myself in a new country, away from my family and friends and all that was familiar to me, feeling that a part of me was missing.

As I am sure you can imagine, the prospect of starting all over, becoming a lawyer again was not one that filled me with enthusiasm. I found myself in a game of snakes and ladders, and though we had climbed the ladder to a safer country with more opportunities, my career went sliding back down to square one.

I have always enjoyed the written word, and at the risk of sounding nerdy, I decided to study for a Master of Arts in Writing *for fun*. There were no career prospects to be gained from this course of study. It was all about nourishing my mind and learning for the enjoyment of it, and to feed my interest in the subject. It was also for the sense of achievement, the feeling of pushing myself forward and reaching a goal.

I firmly believe that we should never stop learning. When you stop learning and growing, you atrophy, and become stuck in an older world where the information and ideas that you had until then acquired, become outdated, and the rest of the world moves on past you. There is always more to learn about the world and yourself. If I can offer you one piece of advice in business and in life, it is to be a life-long learner.

Though I enjoyed my Masters, it did not fill the gap of how I had come to define myself. It would not pay the bills nor provide financial security. There was no career opportunity created in my having earned this degree

There was, therefore, only one thing for it, five years after arriving in Australia I went back to law school to gain the qualifications needed to be a lawyer. When I first attended university after school, it was a time of self-discovery and independence. A time to raise your voice to the things and causes that mattered, and to enjoy the richness of the experience. Starting over did not hold the same allure. I was now older, and a mother of three children, on the brink of separation. The process was certainly more perfunctory than an enjoyable phase in the journey of life.

After law school I had to start my career from scratch. I had to work under the supervision of another lawyer, but I was not, in my experience, a junior lawyer but needed to endure the indignity of being treated as such. In fact, the first lawyer that I worked for was less experienced than me. I later found myself working for two lawyers in two different firms who I ultimately did not respect. As soon as I got the approval from the Legal Services Board to practice law without supervision, my shingle was up again, I was in business for myself. Starting again, as I was beginning my life over after my marriage had ended in divorce.

I'll be very frank with you, it was not easy, it's still a work in progress. I was now on my own, raising my three kids, with no support structure to speak of. Perhaps I should have taken the easy road and found a steady job, but my kids needed me during this transition. I needed to exercise the kind of self-care that I would not have been able to do in a full- time job, with an employer who could possibly add to my stress with their own issues and corporate politics.

No, starting my own business again was the best thing for me, and for my family. It was not just about the money, there are more important things than just money, and I did earn less than what I would have, had I found a full-time job. Even with starting my career again, it would not have been long before I could work my way up and bring my experience as a lawyer to reflect positively upon my employment and position.

I needed the freedom to do what I had to do and to take care of my children. Having my own business was the only answer. Again, I needed to march to the beat of my own drum and call my own shots, and maybe I'm just not 'employee material'. I firmly believe that every cloud has its silver lining. There are opportunities in the most unlikely of places. Starting up a new business, I did not have clients lining the block to see me. New clients came to me slowly and with effort, but fortunately, I knew what to expect having done this all before.

With my area of practice being Wills and Estates, family law, and of course, conveyancing, it was then that I decided to write my book, 'My Life Manual: Information and Messages for my Executors and Loved Ones.', with an Australian and an International edition. Since I was not so busy, my silver lining was that I had the time to write that book. There was something more to me writing these books than merely being a Wills and Estates lawyer. I had a very personal experience in that arena when my own father died. There was so much that I had wanted to ask him, so many things I would have needed his opinion on. On a practical basis, I needed to know how to administer his estate, where to find all his assets and what needed to be done.

I wrote the book knowing what I would have wanted my father to tell me, and what in turn, I would want my own children to know. I wanted my children to know that I loved them so much that I would tell them everything they needed to know, so I created the workbook to do just that. Now my pet passion of writing and the law had come together and produced a book of which I am immensely proud and which I believe can empower other parents to show their undying love and support for their own children and families, to help them through the most difficult time in their relationships with them, the very losing of them.

I still remember the joy of feeling the book in my hands for the very first time, not so dissimilar to feeling the joy of holding your own baby in your arms for the first time. Though, of course, not quite as profound and life altering, but wonderful all the same. Women are creators after all, we feel a deep-down desire to bring something beautiful into the world, to somehow make it a better place. To bring the fruits of our imaginations to life. We do this even in adversity when we feel the world around us pushing us away from our goals and desires, throwing obstacles in our path.

For those of you who have suffered the break down of a marriage, I don't have to explain to you the stress and angst that goes along with it. How things that were once easy seem to take so much more energy to achieve, when all of your energy is spent on keeping your head above water and caring for your family. All the while you question whether you made the right decision in leaving the marriage, and how it may affect your children. There is little energy left over to work on your goals and dreams. Some days it is merely a question of survival.

Thus, my inner nerd was awoken once more. How could I achieve what I wanted to achieve, when there was so much else needing my attention? I read and searched for the answers, and tried to codify a means of reaching my goals, a step by step plan if you will. I did not find a simple answer in one place, so I created it myself. I created what I needed to put in place to achieve what I wanted to achieve and see me going in the direction that I wanted for my life.

So, I wrote my book, "The Dream Catcher: A Journal for Success.' Of course, at that time it wasn't a book but my own structure for meeting my goals, my own outline and workbook for what I needed to consider in putting my plans in motion. It was my notes on what I needed to do to face the challenges and obstacles that would inevitably stand in my way.

As they say, if you want something done properly, do it yourself. My Dream Catcher book helped me to reach my goal of writing my first book, and for navigating the rough terrain of post-divorce life while raising three children. Never let that lack of something stand in your way, if you can't find what you are looking for, be true to your feminine self and create it. That's what makes us unstoppable. We forge our own way and do things the way we want to. Never let society, or anyone else for that matter, tell you how something should be done.

This book was for me and my kids. I surprised them with it for Christmas and loved the look on their faces when they read the dedication of the book to them. I use it for my own planning. While I don't market it actively, I do plan on developing a new edition that I will actively market, fine tuning what I have learnt from using this myself. If I had waited until the book was 'perfect' it would never have been published. Done *is* better than perfect. Just keep moving forward, keep learning, keep improving, never stop trying.

On my path to a new and single life after my divorce, I engaged in a lot of self-reflection. I know many feel the need to jump back into a new relationship and fill that void that has been left by the break up, but I say this, as women we do not need to be in a relationship, we do not *need* to have a man in our lives.

That is not to say that I am opposed to relationships, not at all. The right relationship with the right person is a beautiful and special thing. What I do say is that if you can not be in a healthy relationship with yourself and be comfortable in your own company, to be able to meet your own needs, how are you to have a healthy relationship with someone else who may bring their own baggage to further complicate matters? The first step is to be in a healthy relationship with yourself before pursuing any romantic relationships. I firmly believe that you get out what you put in to something.

What I am saying is that you should not put the key to your own happiness in someone else's pocket. Be strong enough to stand on your own. Do not settle. If you find a man or woman who brings you joy, who lifts you up even further, who makes life better, then go for it. Just never settle, you deserve better than that, we all do.

Women can be very in touch with their emotions, which is a good thing. We allow ourselves to feel. We have not been taught that to express emotion is weak, but in feeling, we can allow the negative emotions of others to bring us down, and in turn, drain us of our energy. For myself at least, I won't settle for just any relationship, I demand a healthy mutually beneficiary relationship based on honesty and respect. If that is not the case, it's not the relationship for me. I hope you will set high standards for yourself, to find relationships that benefit you rather than weigh you down. Don't let the weight of your relationship prevent you for reaching your life goals.

One of the best things that happened to me after my divorce was improving my relationship with myself. Finding my own joy. One of the greatest joys that I found was dancing. I just love it! I'm talking, the Argentine Tango to the Waltz, and just about everything in between. I dance between two to four times a week.

Even going through the worst of my divorce, I never missed a lesson or a class. It was the one constant that kept me going. It was my sacred haven. You can get lost in dance – the movement and the music.

When I was growing up, and this may ring true for many of you, I was told not to 'show off', and never enjoyed drawing attention to myself. You can imagine what the thought of doing dance competitions did to me, even if only at my dance studio. Then there were the medal exams, where I presented between three and five dances to adjudicators from the Australian Dance Society who *judged* me, in a room full of spectators! I was literally terrified, and still get nervous when I perform.

When I first decided to enter studio competitions and do my dance medals, the thought of it filled me with absolute dread. At times I was visibly shaking with nerves. It was tempting to give up and give into my nerves. I mean dancing is supposed to be fun, *right?* Dealing with such terrible nerves was far from fun. So, why do it? I wanted to dance, I love it. I want to progress, and could not do that or feel like I was moving forward without extending myself in this way. I chose to do it because I didn't want to do it. I know that life is best lived outside of my comfort zone. I had to keep pushing myself, knowing that I can feel the fear and do it anyway. At times, conquering that fear was a bigger triumph for me than winning a competition or achieving my medal.

It is therefore my intention to continue dancing, learning more and hopefully improving until I'm well into my 90s. Whether the world is ready for it or not, prepare yourself to see me at ninety in my sparkly diamante encrusted dance dresses, wrinkles included! Likewise, I will see you shaking up the world, doing what you love, never stopping for a moment.

So, after telling you all of this, am I a success? Well, that depends on your definition of success. For me it is a continuum, a constancy of forward movement, of self-improvement as a person and as a business owner. Furthermore. it is being able to look into your own heart and feel a sense of accomplishment and inner peace, that you can not only live with your actions but have authentically sought such achievements.

Only you can define what success means to you and whether you have achieved it. It is whether you have left a legacy worth being proud of. You have a purpose and a vision, and you are reading this to be the best you that there is. To become unstoppable, you need to want it badly enough to push through the discomfort. In searching for the answers, you are closer to achieving your goals.

I fully believe that this also defines an unstoppable woman in business, one who never gives up, is true to herself and her values, and can face down her fears and achieve her desires in spite of those fears.

I truly feel that in spite of my difficulties and hard times, I have become unstoppable and I have achieved things I might not otherwise have achieved. My book, 'My Life Manual', was borne of the terrible time that I had when my father passed away. My passion for dancing arose during my divorce, and in starting my life afresh afterwards, I am happier with the person that I am today.

There are a few things that I believe will tip the scales towards your success in business. For me, it was the following:

- Managing my expenses;
- The pursuit of substance over form;
- Honesty in my dealings with others, owning it;
- Setting up processes that lead to efficiency, especially in repetitive tasks;
- Remembering always WHY I am doing what I'm doing – never forget that;
- Using technology as my friend to automate and streamline;
- Feel empathy for others, understand their pain;
- Never feeling the need to do things the way others have always done them;
- Managing my stress, you do not have to be invincible, just unstoppable;
- Always, always finding time to laugh and have fun.

Most of all I would like to leave you with these three main strategies to achieving unstoppable success in business and in life:

1. Create the right mindset;

Nothing can be achieved without first thinking it so. The first step on your journey to becoming an unstoppable woman in business is to believe it and create goals consistent with that mindset.

2. Never giving up – keep moving forward – your business processes;

You will have obstacles in your way, it is guaranteed. The important thing to do is learn from mistakes, to see the silver lining in all that might otherwise be considered a negative, and create an opportunity from that obstacle.

3. Create your legacy

Create something in your business, and in your life, that you can be proud of and that will leave your family, clients and community better off for your having been there and done what you do. In your planning, keep the idea of building a legacy as an end goal and as a measure of success.

And, if I can offer you one final piece of advice it is this, always be kind to yourself. There are times that you will fail, or things will not go as you might have hoped. In your self-dialogue, take responsibility for your part but never berate yourself, speak to yourself as you would to someone you love. When you can do this, your relationship with yourself is a healthy one, and you will become truly unstoppable, in life and in business.

PART V

NELLA CHIKWE

"Where There Is Purpose There Is Passion, So Pursue It.
Branding Is Your Business, So Protect It."

-Nella Chikwe

BUILD AN EMPIRE, NOT JUST A BUSINESS

BY NELLA CHIKWE

"Where There Is Purpose There Is Passion, So Pursue It.
Branding Is Your Business, So Protect It."

-Nella Chikwe

My journey has enabled me to build an empire of empowerment, enrichment, and elevation in conscious leader's lives, built on the integrity and foundations of emotional intelligence, high-touch transformational experiences and global impact. Building a legacy and an empire is how I got to know my own formidable strength. I learned during my years of insurmountable adversities in life that I was not built to break. It prepared me for my pursuit of purpose. I learned I was built to be fierce, fearless and UNSTOPPABLE. Greatness was my birthright!

My years of setbacks prepared, shaped and led me to the abundance I am experiencing today in all areas of my life and businesses. Abundance can be interpreted by people in many different ways.

The biggest block to receiving abundance is the feeling of being unworthy and undeserving. Abundance is your natural birthright and when you decide to accept it for yourself, you will attract like-minded individuals.As for me, I acknowledged my abundance by building a wealth of resolve, emotional intelligence, increasing my IP assets, having a millionaire mindset, financial astuteness, encouraging my inner circle and most importantly, an unwavering spirit and belief in my divine calling. Allowing for divine guidance to orchestrate my business steps with flowing strategies that successfully transformed the scope of my businesses. I began turning my *Purpose into Profit!*

Finding your divine purpose is the first key to acquiring abundance. Why, you might ask? When you find your divine purpose, it will guide you to step out and stand out to successfully SOAR in life and business. It first starts with a successful plan for you to build the principles and foundations to propel your purpose for greater influence and impact. Everything relies on having an effective plan followed by unwavering execution, powered by a relentless drive to carry out the vision until victory is won.

Fortune is in the *follow-up* and offering *high-touch* service, without diverting from your vision or compromising on your voice, values and visibility. This is the second most powerful principle I have mastered in my businesses, which is quite often overlooked in the modern and ever-changing digital age we live in today!

The road to entrepreneurship is not for the faint-hearted; it's not all glory. It requires great sacrifice and zeal but offers substantial rewards. It was certainly great strength training for mental endurance, resilience, will-power and determination. If you survive the rocky journey you will certainly come out the other end a mighty warrior. I had experienced countless of setbacks, losses, great disappointment, despair, delays and unfortunate dealings with unethical people who lacked integrity in their professional practice.

In the early hours of the 15th of May 2016, following the recent loss of my mother-in-law came the pivotal moment when *I said YES* to my divine purpose; Pioneering the Unstoppable Woman Of Purpose Global Movement. I had every reason to postpone my purpose, delay my destiny and neglect my newfound passion for helping spirited, high-achieving women increase their value and influence globally. I decided to honour my divine calling and knew there and then I was on a path to creating a remarkable empire, not just another business.

Birthing a global movement to create change, inspire, influence and make an impactful difference in the world is certainly *not* for the faint-hearted. A season of setbacks; being misunderstood, over-looked, undervalued, defamed and being an under-dog made my new mission all the worthwhile. I was determined to be an advocate for conscious women leaders and allow their voice to be heard, by sharing their story through writing, publishing and speaking on my global stage. Backed by years of preparation investing in my personal and professional education, experience and elevation, I began my journey to educate, empower and elevate aspiring conscious women leaders to become Unstoppable Women of Purpose.

My ambitious goal was to create a lasting legacy that would triumph over tribulations and create transformational testimonies of great impact for many aspiring women leaders globally. I never classified myself as a professional writer, as my passion lies in being an international speaker, inspiring change from the stage. Neverthe-less, as I embarked on my vision, I was reassured by divine grace that my Maker would be by my side assisting me as He inspires greatness.

As a business marketing graduate, I knew from the early days of establishing my businesses over 18 years ago that I was my own brand, and it was my mission to build and protect it during its expansion. I knew I was onto something BIG; I knew my purpose was going to create a global impact. The spiritual anointing that is in my life got me through the chaos I endured to get where I am today.

The mere fact that you are reading this, that you are here right now, about to absorb the essence of my success story in business is no coincidence. Firstly, allow me to share some of what it has taken me to be an unstoppable woman in business, like so many other success stories of global entrepreneurs. Success is not by chance or luck. For there to be great WINS in business, it means many great losses have been endured, ultimately sharpening the entrepreneur into what the world finally gets to witness - their success state in business today! Success is earned through sheer diligence, determination and drive, challenging you to gain clarity and conviction in your purpose as an innovative, visionary entrepreneur. Being an entrepreneur requires one to be UNSTOPPABLE.

VISIONARY WOMAN, ARE YOU READY TO SOAR IN BUSINESS?

In conquering my divine global assignment with confidence in elevating conscious leaders internationally, I am joined by 13 unstoppable women in my collective three-volume series. Thus, sharing their stories and success of being unapologetically unstoppable. It is a divine moment in time. I have been prepared for such a time as this, for such a time as NOW!

Embarking on your transformational journey of becoming an unstoppable woman in business is a testament to my sheer unwavering belief in my global vision. A vision that was birthed just over two years ago has now materialized into eight global published books, with four completed volumes out of a 24-part series. I am invested in creating an anointed global anthology; a masterpiece that will leave you awe-inspired to step out, stand out and soar in business.

This anthology has already influenced and impacted countless women around the world prior to it being published. I am confident that this book will also launch your transformational journey to becoming an *Unstoppable Woman In Business*. Right now, give yourself permission to experience the next catapult level in business. You deserve it. You were created to walk through this life and be victorious doing it. All that is required is faith the size of a mustard seed and the floodgates will open. The only person that can stop you right now is you! The process is all about taking that first step.

FORMIDABLE STRENGTH OF
REALIZING THE VISION

As an empowered and unstoppable woman of purpose, I have nevertheless coped with decades of misfortunes, financial and emotional turmoil. I have experienced contractual droughts in business, disservice, disempowerment and disappointments. Despite all I had endured, I refused to crumble. Nor did I allow it to stop my success in achieving my dreams, desires and divine destiny.

"Strength grows in the moments when you think you can't go on, but you keep going anyway."

-Unknown

I dug deep and didn't allow the distractions of my current circumstances to slow me down. In fact, I made conscious decisions to use determination to push through when faced with giants of adversity, regardless of the drama that could have deterred me from living to the fullest of my divine purpose. I had decided not to be defeated or allow those disturbances to define me nor shape my victorious destiny. Lesson learned was to focus on the journey to success, as that's when you are truly living. It develops character, and tests your drive and resolve.

Smile in the face of adversity, as it shapes your story to share and inspire others to greatness. Dance with your fears. Fears will inevitably creep into your life and business, make no mistake about it. But how you handle it is what matters. The meaning you give to what happens to you is what matters most. Never underestimate the power of the mind, as it can create paradigm shifts. I encourage you to feel the fear, dance with it and conquer it! Celebrate your accomplishments, successes and achievements thus far. Travel the road to success with your head held high, your shoulders back and stand tall knowing you are victorious! People need YOU, all of YOU. Your presence, your listening skills, your brain, your skills, your compassion, not just your message.

As women, we lead in so many areas of life: being a wife, mother, daughter, friend, CEO, visionary, entrepreneur and mentor. But one thing you should always remember is; "a great leader's courage to fulfil her vision comes from passion, not position, *so don't get so caught up on all of the titles you hold that you miss what you were destined to do and be*". It's time to tap into your power, embrace your passion, remain positive, be Unstoppable and LEAD with purpose. You have been filled by the Spirit with something that is getting ready to bring you into a season of longevity, legacy building, fruitfulness and fulfilment.

Your life has purpose
Your story is important
Your dreams count
Your voice needs to be heard
You were born to make an impactful difference
You are your Brand
Build your Empire
Create a Legacy that stands the test of time
Share Your Story as You... SOAR in Business.

"Legacy is not leaving something for people, it's leaving something in people."

- Peter Strople

I know the source and sustenance of manifestation to building an empire is an inside job. It was through the interminable twists and turns in life that allowed me to strengthen my emotional and spiritual muscle, build character, gain more wisdom and ultimately allowed me to turn my adversities into abundance. My pain into purpose and my purpose into passion. Placing me on the road to spiritual, emotional and financial abundance. Leading me to my divine purpose where I found my gifts of genius, greatness and passion for life. I never underestimated my worth nor the value I'd bring to the world. While life had a way of trying to distract me with daily complex curveballs during my years of tribulations, yet the still, small voice of God would say to me, *"I have placed seeds within you that contain gifts and talents. It looks small right now but give it time; it will prosper."*

In every season of our life and business, we are always being divinely guided. There is a capable warrior inside of you that wants to be unleashed. To create, build, expand, elevate, inspire, influence, impact, soar and to do so much more than just exist.

I sharpened my leadership, communication, negotiation and selling skills through educating, empowering, elevating and transforming many visionary lives and businesses. I am a woman who is highly intuitive, strategic and masterful in igniting the greatness in others. I revel in enabling their light to shine bright like a diamond. To increase their value and influence globally by sharing their story; their voice matters!

I encourage you to expand, elevate and empower yourself to do more of what you love, so you can maximize your potential to fulfil your purpose, be of greater service, leave a legacy, and be that history-maker you were born to be.

WHAT ARE YOU WAITING FOR?

The dreams that you were about to give up on are turning into diamonds and pearls in your hands. If you know you are wired and destined to be an entrepreneur, then what are you waiting on to elevate your brand, business and message to all-new heights?

- *How can you expand your empire?*
- *Don't you think it's your time to think global, not just local?*
- *Are you willing to do what is required to be a serial entrepreneur?*
- *What if you knew for certain that a particular change in your life and business would lead to greater freedom, fulfillment and joy?*
- *What if you could put aside any fear of failure, disappointment, or rejection?*
- *What would it take for you to more fully embrace your power to pursue your purpose and create a lasting legacy?*

*"It's TIME to Step Out, Stand Out and SOAR
in Life and Business."*

-Nella Chikwe

Garner the courage to:

- *Believe change is possible*
- *Trust yourself to change*
- *Move from the familiar to the unfamiliar*
- *Open your mind to new possibilities*
- *Cooperate with the process of change*
- *Feel vulnerable during times of change*
- *Let go of old habits*
- *Face new, unforeseen challenges*
- *Be the change you want to see in the world*

To build an empire requires a level of business acumen, seeking a professional team of experts, innovation, drive, determination, and diligence. It also needs a whole lot of focused passion to help propel your plan into a substantial, resourceful and impactful pathway to enrich and empower people, whilst ultimately profiting in business. Yes, there are financial trusts, deeds and specific legalities which are vital to be established by licensed professional experts to help you structure and set up your business foundation. Doing this correctly allows for business and financial growth whilst protecting the designated directors and beneficiaries nominated. Do not be tempted to skip this significant step in the process! I would encourage you to entrust this duty of establishing company trust structures to the experts in this field; no unstoppable woman in business neglects the integral importance of establishing these frameworks correctly. It's all part of the process of transforming purpose to profit.

My main focus in this chapter about building an empire, not *just* a business; is to draw attention to the predominant strategies I used when setting out to fulfil my life's purpose in the midst of running my several other companies. I work in the specialist areas of: sales and marketing, wealth advisory, business consultancy, in addition to global publishing and soon will establish a business partnership with my husband, who is a Barrister. It is our intention to expand our group of companies and establish our own law practice where he can thrive in his purpose and serve the greater community with his area of expertise.

We plan to use our children's middle names as our company name and trust, just as I did for my global publishing company; *Winston Cartier Publishing*. A personal element we apply when expanding our business empire and company trusts. Leaving a legacy of significance is our main motivation in building a business of value and merit. Focusing on the power in people with integrity and compassion is what we aim to achieve in all of our business ventures, partnerships and projects. They are the key motivators to which we hold tight and value in our everyday business practices.

THE FIVE KEY SUCCESS STRATEGIES TO APPLY IN BUSINESS:

1. **Intentions**
2. **Inspire**
3. **Influence**
4. **Integrity**
5. **Impact**

1. Intentions

Set clear goals, boundaries and value-added intentions for *what, how, when* and *why* you want to achieve the desired business goal. Have intentions that are in total alignment with your business values and missions. Monitor the performance of your goals and intentions regularly to ensure the integrity of the intentions aren't being compromised. Having a clear roadmap of your business plan helps to keep your intentions concise, clear and compliant to your core beliefs, values and marketing message.

2. Inspire

Aspire to inspire should be your primary objective in business. Know that there is power in people. Without loyal clients to invest in your product or purchase your professional services, your business will remain volatile and as a result your profits will feel the pinch. Ensure your core message and marketing strategies are designed to inspire your target market, providing them with valuable insights at all times. Allow the ideal client to become brand loyal and spread the good word of your company to their circle of people. As the saying goes; *"word spreads fast"*.

3. Influence

Clients who have received great benefit from your product and service will ultimately be influenced by you and your company. They will surely come back, desiring more of what your company has to offer. This builds brand loyalty and will enable those clients you are called to serve to receive great return on their investment by way of offering exceptional service and quality control. Receiving client feedback is a great way to ascertain the level of influence your company has on the overall client experience. It enables you to review the feedback and re-evaluate your processes in order to keep your intentions on point, inspiration values in check and level of positive influence for your clients on high!

4. Integrity

YOU are your brand and it's your business to protect it! The more you create value, inspire your target market and provide cutting-edge, superior customer service, your clients will surely become brand loyal. They will recommend and refer your business services to others in their sphere of influence. It is imperative to have integrity in your business practise. Say what you mean and mean what you say. To never over promise on your services. The integral and best form of principle I apply in business is to under-promise and over-deliver! This ensures I am providing a WOW-factor to all of my clients in the professional services my companies render.

5. Impact

Repeat business from valued clients wanting MORE of what you have to offer, is a clear sign of brand loyalty. Providing clients with continual valued services that is both inspirational and innovative should be your focal point in creating mass impact. Critical analysis, client feedback and testimonials from clients is a clear indication and way of ascertaining the level of impact your company has in the marketplace. Profit and Loss statements are a great barometer of HOW much value you are giving out into the marketplace. Figures don't lie; they are black and white. Numbers in a balance sheet are a clear way of judging how you are transforming your purpose to profit. Keep your eye on your creating VALUE for your clients, serving them with the utmost respect, heart and integrity and you will soon witness your back balance grow FAT. Remember, you are building an empire, *not just a business*. THINK long-haul, think legacy, not just a one-off transaction. Treating every client as if they are your only one is a great way of maintaining humility in your business practice and keeping the level of integrity high. Think about how you would love to be treated and increase that expectation by ten! It is a valuable principle to apply when creating an empire. Some food for thought for you.

Allow me to illustrate why I know that this is the season for you to step out, stand out and soar in business. Firstly, because you are not alone. It is the season for women around the globe like you to rise, stand tall and overcome adversity with confidence and certainty. To use your past pain as fuel to push and pull you into your purpose. That is where your ultimate success, joy, fulfillment and great victory lies.

As a visionary, when you're birthing an expansive billion-dollar DREAM; you must be prepared to be perceived by some as peculiar. Your dream, like any childbirth, requires to be fully formed and developed. Your vision needs lungs; oxygen for you to breathe life, light and hope into the world. Life of bountiful enriching possibilities and golden opportunities. For you to be holding tight to this masterful piece of work, it is a miracle. Nevertheless, those vivid experiences were designed to grow something *great* within me. I knew I couldn't have delivered that precious dream, if I'd chosen to live a life of mediocrity. A life where everything would be easy, simple, and where it didn't require me to stretch without being pulled, pushed or prodded!

Now, that which was lying dormant – my *Greatness*; has come alive right before my eyes. A substantive life, so majestic that is not only purposeful but impactful. It is what I train, equip and empower visionary woman of purpose to live for. To set their standard of greatness to a whole new epic dimension.

It is time to release the greatness within you that you have been holding. It is your time to step out on faith and believe it is possible. When it is your time, nothing or no one can stop you. Only YOU can detour yourself from your purpose. We are fearfully and wonderfully made women of God. When the world says *"No"*, God says *"Go!"* When man turns his back on you, God turns His face towards you and says, *"No more hesitation, my daughter; it's time to pursue my will in your life…It's time to allow the divine flow to propel your purpose to your promised land of prosperity and profitability in life and business!"*

Remember you are your own brand. Your brand is your business. When you're prospering in life it should overflow into your business profits. Why, might you say? It is simple; there is no separation between you, your brand and your business. You are ONE! Allow me to paint a clear picture; a recent inappropriate statement by the CEO of a Fortune-500 company reflected negatively on the company and its stock. In essence, your behaviour as a CEO can positively or negatively have an immediate effect on your company within the market place. So, in short, as a visionary, founder and CEO of your company, you need to set your intentions right, before considering establishing any business, expanding or scaling your business.

Continually working on your personal development is key and fundamental to elevating any business to a catalyst level. It's a culmination of your inner work, values, integrity in your personal life and mindset mastering that will significantly reflect your efforts in your business practices, performance, productivity and profitability. Sales growth and customer brand loyalty are all part and parcel of getting the structure and systems correct. Mastering your mindset, knowing how you project yourself on a personal level carries weight in building your brand, business and empire. It is imperative to get it right from the onset.

"Winning is an inside job."

-John Maxwell

For most of my twenties and early to mid-thirties my vision for my future was blurred. That period left deep scars which were caused by financial uncertainty and stolen IP from former business alliances lacking integrity and creditability. Unsurmountable lack of contracts, lack of direction and clarity followed. Feeling frightened, abandoned, bewildered and confused, I despaired. These are experiences I conquered and have earned me the honour of being an unstoppable woman of purpose.

In the midst of our countless disappointments, even though I felt emotionally bankrupted, I refused to give up. I was not prepared to lose everything we had acquired because of unsupportive people or situations out of our control, no matter how hard the road was. I surrendered all, trusting in my vision and knew in my heart and soul that I would overcome great uncertainty with confidence and conviction. I had an unwavering spirit to see it through until the finishing line, no matter what! I knew I was an unstoppable woman of purpose destined to be more, do more and no longer play small! My mission was to inspire empowering positive change, influence many aspiring, conscious leaders and create an impactful difference around the globe.

THE POWER OF PURPOSE AND PROFITABILITY

Others experience adversity in their journey and quite often stop in their tracks, paralysed by their pain in pursuit of purpose. I have mastered my mindset through years of adversity, advancing in my higher education, reading countless books and having supportive mentors along my journey. I had gained a reputation among my inner circle that I made "unbearable situations" look gracious. I managed this because of the power of the mind and how I value myself, my vision and purpose.

I am an unstoppable woman in business as I have an unbreakable, unapologetic and unstoppable spirit of belief in my purpose, vision and values. I choose to visualise the finishing line before I embark on a new endeavour and don't waver when the going gets tough. I hold the dream tight to my heart until it materializes. To achieve the goal, I keep my eyes open to all the opportunities and embrace every challenge that brings me closer to my purpose. My life's journey has ultimately brought me closer to YOU!

You will learn to shine when you experience the fiery furnace of setbacks or the overwhelming stress of problems. Discouragement and failure are only stepping stones to success. Every setback you've experienced has only been progress. *There is strength in you. I want you to begin manifesting each step in your life. That will create a greater prosperity reality for you.*

The Five "P's" that will lead you to your business elevation and expansion and help you on your way to building an empire, not *just* a business is; a are clear sense of *Purpose, Professional Experts to* support you to propel your progress into new heights, *Plan of Action, a heightened Passion, and roadmap to achieving Profitability* as you prosper and create impact in business.

SET OUT TO SOAR

Part of my preparation for sustaining success and overcoming adversity in embracing my purpose, valuing my greater gifts and being warrior-like lies in protecting my 'WHY.' Ask yourself some fundamental questions; Why have you been chosen for your unique purpose? What are your motivating drivers? Who is it affecting and impacting? What gets you up before dawn, raring to face the day? Remember, whatever you unconsciously or consciously give meaning to, it will inevitably take on the nature of the meaning you give to it. Why not interpret everything as a gift? Guard your tongue and heart. It can lead you to places of compromise, competing and comparing.

"Above all else, guard your heart, for everything you do flows from it."

-Proverbs 4:23

MASTER A MILLIONAIRE MINDSET

Today, I encourage you to break any stronghold in your life and business that has tried to quiet the greatness of your destiny, living on the inside. If you want to achieve success, it starts from within. Adversity is designed to deposit something within you that you can't get when everything is easy and going your way!

At first, it may irritate you, like a grain of sand within the soft interior of an oyster. How you give it meaning, how you treat it, decides whether you have a deep, unhealed wound or a glowing pearl. Every challenge you've been through has deposited something in you; what will you do with it?

Outrageous success comes from thinking different, being different and having the bold confidence to always do what feels right in your heart. You will understand the importance of surrounding yourself with wisdom. You will begin to reflect on your past success instead of seeing failure. You will begin to change your scenery to inspire growth in your life. You will begin to break the routine as you do things differently.

This is the season where you are developing your emotional and spiritual muscles to push forward to prepare for your next heightened level of success. It is important that you understand that tests only prepare you for the next level! They sharpen your character and gives you clarity and conviction in pursuit of purpose. My desire for you is that you will be poised for the remaining year ahead. To maximize your unique potential and fulfil a divine purpose for an extraordinary, influential, and abundant life!

"Elevating & Accelerating Minds to Manifest Victory."

-Nella Chikwe

How Do You Want To Be Remembered?

LEGACY Building; it's not just what you did, but the thoughts of YOU in someone else's mind that should be your focus. Live each day in the way you want to be remembered.

It's time; the world needs you NOW. Our world is roaring, ready and righteous, for your return to a purposeful and prosperous life. There is an almighty shift happening and you are at the core of it. YOU have free will to make a choice of finding purpose, meaning and reward from the transformational journey ahead. I challenge you to dig deep, find that confidence, clarity and the courageous warrior within.

You are setting up to reap a harvest that you've only dreamed about. It's time for you to pursue the dream! Embrace being THE UNSTOPPABLE WOMAN OF PURPOSE that longs to be unleashed. Be Bold, Confident and Obedient to Your Purpose; Knowing It Is Uniquely Designed For YOU!

THE UNSTOPPABLE WOMAN OF PURPOSE
GLOBAL ANTHOLOGY SERIES

Upcoming 24 Series

As you have embarked on your quest to become an UNSTOPPABLE WOMAN IN BUSINESS; in reading this anthology of inspiring and empowering stories of global women leaders.

I encourage you to follow the GLOBAL MOVEMENT. Its mission is to continue to equip, enrich and empower YOU to lead an unstoppable life and business with purpose. To yield the visionary woman with our upcoming resourceful and inspirational series will ultimately support your complete transformational journey embodying personally, professionally and spiritually.

Continue your transformational journey with the upcoming 3rd and 4th Volume of the 24 Series.

The Unstoppable Woman Of Unwavering Faith
Volume 3 of 24 Series

The Unstoppable Woman Of Audacious Confidence
Volume 4 of 24 Series

A Special Invitation

We have a global opportunity for Unstoppable Women who are in full alignment with their purpose. We are here to have your VOICE heard. As your Story Matters!

This opportunity is for feminine expert and thought leaders, who desire to share their expertise, experiences and wisdom. You are welcome to connect with us, as we are happy to share more about this global opportunity to provide you expansive exposure. JOIN our movement where visionary women collaborate and courageously share their success stories of conquering challenges and situations in life and business with confidence and certainty.

Each year there will be three (3) anthologies focusing on *Life, Business* and *Spirituality*. The series totalling 24 series will embody the mind, body and spirit of the visionary woman desiring to do more and be more and no longer play small.

"An abundant purposeful life filled with Purpose, Passion and Prosperity AWAITS!"

-Nella Chikwe

MISSION

Nella's mission is to empower the lives of every visionary entrepreneurial woman, to lead successful lives and businesses with *confidence, certainty and conviction;* whilst being *unstoppable in her expansive thinking, creativity, giving & living.*

Creating a global movement of empowerment in women; The Unstoppable Woman of Purpose. Reaching women globally who desire to unleash their inner-fierce self, embrace their gifts with feminine grace, ignite their passion, value their worth and ultimately step into that UNSTOPPABLE Woman of Purpose they were meant to be. Who will then unapologetically charge her power and catapult in life and business!

VISION

For every visionary woman to live life on purpose with passion. To prosper in life and profit in business, being spiritual, smart and substantive. As the world is waiting for her to INSPIRE, INFLUENCE and make an IMPACT to those she is called to serve.

To value the importance of genuine connection, contribution and divine collaboration within the scope of impact that is inimical to competition and comparison.

To inspire greatness in women so that they can become that formidable force of possibility and an unapologetic confident leader. She will step into her greatness, become unstoppable in pursuing her purpose with passion, who charges her power both financially and emotionally. Ultimately allowing her **Voice, Vision & Visibility** to make an impactful difference around the globe.

<u>Accompanying Product Series – Vol. 2</u>
Available from online retail stores

The Unstoppable Woman In Business
Accompanied Workbook, Vol.2

An accompanying workbook to the global anthology series – Vol 2. The Unstoppable Woman In Business.

Nella Chikwe with global women leaders share their successful strategies of how they have stepped out and soared in business. Leading to inspire and influence aspiring conscious leaders. The intention of the workbook is to provide a strategic framework to self-discover and align the visionary woman to her purposeful, substantive and prosperous business.

Would love to hear how this anthology has helped to empower YOU?

Testimonies may be sent to:

Email:
enquiries@theunstoppablewomanofpurpose.com
Website: theunstoppablewomanofpurpose.com

Follow us:
Facebook:
facebook.com/theunstoppablewomanofpurpose
facebook.com/winstoncartierpublishing

PROVERBS 31 WOMAN

"**1** The sayings of King Lemuel—an inspired utterance his mother taught him. **2** Listen, my son! Listen, son of my womb! Listen, my son, the answer to my prayers! **3** Do not spend your strength on women, your vigor on those who ruin kings. **4** It is not for kings, Lemuel— it is not for kings to drink wine, not for rulers to crave beer, **5** lest they drink and forget what has been decreed and deprive all the oppressed of their rights **6** Let beer be for those who are perishing, wine for those who are in anguish! **7** Let them drink and forget their poverty and remember their misery no more. **8** Speak up for those who cannot speak for themselves, for the rights of all who are destitute. **9** Speak up and judge fairly; defend the rights of the poor and needy. **10** A wife of noble character who can find? She is worth far more than rubies. **11** Her husband has full confidence in her and lacks nothing of value. **12** She brings him good, not harm, all the days of her life. **13** She selects wool and flax and works with eager hands. **14** She is like the merchant ships, bringing her food from afar. **15** She gets up while it is still night; she provides food for her family and portions for her female servants. **16** She considers a field and buys it; out of her earnings she plants a vineyard. **17** She sets about her work vigorously; her arms are strong for her tasks. **18** She sees that her trading is profitable and her lamp does not go out at night. **19** In her hand she holds the distaff and grasps the spindle with her fingers. **20** She opens her arms to the poor and extends her hands to the needy. **21** When it snows, she has no fear for her household; for all of them are clothed in scarlet. **22** She makes coverings for her bed; she is clothed in fine linen and purple. **23** Her husband is respected at the city gate, where he takes his seat among the elders of the land. **24** She makes linen garments and sells them and supplies the merchants with sashes. **25** She is clothed with strength and dignity; she can laugh at the days to come. **26** She speaks with wisdom and faithful instruction is on her tongue. **27** She watches over the affairs of her household and does not eat the bread of idleness. **28** Her children arise and call her blessed; her husband also, and he praises her: **29** "Many women do noble things, but you surpass them all." **30** Charm is deceptive and beauty is fleeting; but a woman who fears the LORD is to be praised. **31** Honor her for all that her hands have done and let her works bring her praise at the city gate."

-Proverbs 31 1:31(NIV)

WHAT IS THE MINDSET OF AN UNSTOPPABLE, PROVERBS 31 WOMAN?

An Unstoppable, Proverbs 31 Woman... knows her worth and values her divine gifts. She is confident in her own skin, she is inspiring, empowering and doesn't settle for anything less. She loves luxury and the finest things that life can offer, she gives life her absolute best. She pushes through beyond limits; she never gives up and strives for excellence in all that she does personally and professionally. She uplifts, encourages & empowers people around her; no matter what her present circumstances dictates. She is selfless, caring, compassionate and generous. She will always rise to every occasion and leaves her empowering imprint wherever she goes.

She knows her greatest purpose to make a positive difference in the lives of many. Loves to help and see people happy. She is the light in any dark situation, she is a leader, trend setter, game changer and believes she can turn her mess into a greater message that will help many. She is experienced, a true professional and loves up levelling herself. She values family & friends. She practices daily in creating memorable moments, she believes in constant personal development. She is passionate, enthusiastic, has strong business acumen, she is thorough, very creative, an expert in direct sales, a strong negotiator and not afraid to provide clear boundaries within her business practice. Keep fighting until victory is WON!

She is daring in her business approach and a dangerous dreamer. She acknowledges her gifts to inspire, empower and ignite people's inner calling, passion and purpose on fire. She is influential and willing to share her journey of heartache, vulnerabilities, challenges days of despair to give others a sense of HOPE. She is willing to share her MESS and turn into a strong MESSAGE that will touch many around the globe. She has so much experience and wisdom to share.

AN UNSTOPPABLE, PURPOSEFUL PROVERBS 31 WOMAN IS;

VIRTUOUS

She seeks His will for her life and follows his ways.
She acknowledges her divine gifts and values
her worth as she graciously serves Him.
She earnestly embraces her purpose
with all her heart, mind and soul.

1. LOYAL: Staying loyal to her husband, never wavering his faith and trust in her. She protects, provides and pursues in her wifely duties effortlessly for all the days of her life. Empowering, supporting and motivating her husband to be the best man that he can be in the name of Jesus.

2. HARDWORKING: She is steadfast and works diligently with eagerness, resolve and consistency. She doesn't entertain laziness or procrastination and is always able to provide for her family. She is an early riser maintaining a constructive routine for her and her families life.

3. ENDURANCE: She is committed to complete her assignment until full completion. She graciously hustles. Endures many late nights and early mornings to get the work done, no matter what it takes. She endures hard times and continues to press in and push through until victory is won.

4. STRENGTH: She has palpable energy. She is strong spiritually, emotionally and physically. She pursues her purpose with passion and optimism.

5. INDUSTRIOUS: She is multi-skilled, multi-talented and values her skills, talents and experiences. She uses all her divine gifts to the fullest and leaves no stone unturned. She is an optimist opportunist.

6. ENTREPRENEURIAL: She is a visionary and a provider for her family. She earns an income and seizes wise investments and opportunities to expand her reach.

7. FINANCIALLY ASTUTE: She is diligent with financing and budgeting. She is intelligent, resourceful and experienced to handle money and wealth accumulation. She is wise and discerning when spending and invests wisely.

8. CHARITABLE: She extends a helping hand to her community and assists the needy. She is humble and meek. Welcomes everyone with open arms and is non-judgmental.

9. STYLISH: She has an innate flair for elegance, class and style. She values quality not quantity and values quality workmanship.

10. HONORABLE: She is integral, committed to her purpose, whilst respecting and valuing people.

11. THOUGHTFUL: She takes her families thoughts, feelings and opinions with confidence certainty and conviction. She makes sure everyone is taken care of before herself. Her putting herself before anyone that she cares about. Pleasing others and God is what she lives for.

12. DRIVEN: Staying true to duties as a mother and wife; getting up in the middle of the night, tending to her children and husband. She stands tall and keeps pushing through.

13. BRILLIANT: Finding new and upcoming ways to provide. She takes leaps and bounds by learning and investing so that her family can have means they so desire.

14. PROVIDER: She provides food, shelter, clothing and education for her family. Creating and paving a way for a purpose filled and abundant life.

15. INTUITIVE: She wears strength and dignity on her heart and laughs at the days to come. Being unstoppable and trusting herself to make the right decisions for her and her family.

16. FAITHFUL: She is just, speaks wisdom and truth. She follows His faithful instructions, being unstoppable and unwavering in her faith. Having faith in oneself and God to push through the tough times. She joins her children and husband together as one in her pursuit to purpose.

17. OBEDIENT: She is a woman who fears the lord; for that, she shall be praised.

18. RESILIENCE: She rides through the storms of life with unwavering faith. She is steadfast on her purpose and will not be pulled or pushed off course.

19. WISE: She is deep, thought-provoking and insightful. She is well-rounded, educated and spiritually substantive. She thinks before she speaks and does so with grace and kindness.

20. PROSPEROUS: She is a conqueror, a victor, an investor and an unstoppable woman of purpose. She diligently monetizes her intellectual property and divine gift to ultimately inspire, influence and impact those she is called to serve. Her unstoppable work ethics, dedication, unwavering faith, relentless determination and commitment to follow through with her purpose is acknowledged by God and her family.

The challenge is staying consistent every day in having a disciplined balanced lifestyle and maintaining a high level of work ethics, integrity, loyalty, determination, resilience, resolve, intuition, planning, execution, faithfulness, obedience, wisdom, discernment, patience, compassion, brilliance, selflessness, belief, love and expansive vision. Even if you aren't a believer these 20 attributes are crucial in finding a meaningful and purpose filled life. All God wants is for His children to be filled with love, joy and peace. Never forget, you are worthy, you are enough and you are UNSTOPPABLE!

I LAY IN YOUR POWER

I decree and declare this blessing unto you on this very day, as this is declared by the lord your savior that your experience on this day will only be of goodness. I lay in your power that today brings you divine opportunities and may your best of today be your worst of your tomorrow. I declare this moment in time to be your defining moment in becoming an unmovable unwavering, unshakeable unstoppable woman of purpose. May your soul be lit on fire and you establish your divine purpose. May you embrace your god given assignment and speak the word of the lord. I lay in your power blessings upon your life as you leave your legacy.

May joy, peace, prosperity and success be abundant in your life, business and ministry. May you be memorialized. May your ideas, creations, and services be high in demand. May your presence be felt amongst the influential and powerful. I lay in your power many victories against the enemy in your life. May your life be fruitful in all that you desire. I lay in your power all that has been given unto you as your divine destiny. May money be of no issue or worry in your life. May you have the heart to be a godly humanitarian, giving unto those who cannot repay you. May you never lack productivity in your life.

May your family be favored by God. May they never be homeless or go without their needs. I lay in your power to teach others how to be the head and not the tail. I lay in your power to strengthen the inner man. May you continue to dream big and teach others. I lay in your power to be the first and never the last. May you experience supernatural suddenlies and shifts in your life, business and witness in others. May the light always set your pathway.

I lay in your power to embrace God's fullness and to be able to live life to your full potential. May you live mortgage free. May you set and achieve honorable goals. May you never settle for less than you deserve. May you forever be able to stay laser focused. I lay in your power the gift to achieve leaps and bounds over all walls and obstacles in your way. In the name of Jesus, I decree and declare your life to be supernaturally changed and empowered from this day forward; as your new divine unstoppable self.

Nella Chikwe

ABOUT THE FOUNDER

THE UNSTOPPABLE WOMAN OF PURPOSE
GLOBAL MOVEMENT

NELLA CHIKWE

Global Leadership Advisor, Publisher, Speaker,
Intl. Bestselling Author & Entrepreneur

Founder of The Unstoppable Woman Of Purpose Global
Movement and Winston Cartier Publishing

"Revolutionizing lives, by elevating minds."

–Nella Chikwe

Nella Chikwe is an influencer with an innate ability to elevate passionate high achieving leaders to increase their personal power, value, visibility and influence globally. Helping conscious entrepreneurs to get recognised as experts and leaders in their industry.

Nella is a qualified Financial Planner, Global Speaker, Leadership Advisor, International Bestselling Author, Publisher with graduate degrees in business, marketing and finance. She has been in the global speaking arena for over 20 years sharing her exponential knowledge in specialty areas of thought leadership, entrepreneurship and wealth creation. A highly respected by her peers in the property, financial planning and finance industry. Her inner passion is contagious as she delivers a unique, insightful, captivating and engaging presentation.

She actively advises corporations, medium enterprises and entrepreneurs in areas of leadership, professional development, sales and marketing. Culminating in increased performance, productivity and profitability.

Nella's wealth of professional expertise includes; thought leadership, business advisory, wealth creation, property investment, forex, financial planning, sales and marketing. A quintessential leader that will catapult company visions to another influential level.

Founder of Winston Cartier Publishing & The Unstoppable Woman Of Purpose Global Movement. Nella has been empowering conscious leaders to increase their value and influence globally by writing, speaking, publishing. In addition, to providing a global educational and transformational platform for women entrepreneurs through her Luxe Mastermind Global Retreats.

Contact Nella:

Email:

nella@nellachikwe.com

Websites:

nellachikwe.com

winstoncartierpublishing.com

theunstoppablewomanofpurpose.com

Facebook:

facebook.com/nellachikwespeaks

facebook.com/winstoncartierpublishing

facebook.com/theunstoppablewomanofpurpose

Closed Group:

facebook.com/groups/BEmpoweredVisionaryWomenOfPurpose

Instagram:

instagram.com/nellachikwe

Twitter:

twitter.com/nellachikwe

LinkedIn:

linkedin.com/in/nellachikwe

Youtube:

youtube.com/nellachikwe

ABOUT THE CO-AUTHORS

The Co-Authors are listed in alphabetical order by surname. They are not listed in order of chapter sequence.

Sarah Griffiths (Aust)
Melissa Brown Odazie (USA)
Hazel Todd (Aust)
Veronika Whyte (Aust)

SARAH GRIFFITHS

Peak Performance Strategist, Executive Coach, Entrepreneur, Author & Speaker

"Change Yourself, Change Your beliefs, Change Your Life."

-Sarah Griffiths

Sarah Griffiths is a multi-award nominated, 7-figure serial entrepreneur, who uses her extensive experience in the area of peak performance, leading with emotional intelligence to help corporate executives and SME companies grow and scale their businesses.

Following a stellar career in the corporate sector, she actively runs three profitable companies.

As a conscious leader, Sarah actively engages her skills of expertise in the areas of mindset mastery and thought leadership, using NLP and RTT modalities in her coaching and business advisory. She is a passionate specialist in cutting-edge therapy, using this to help her clients receive rapid results in mindset matters and overcoming limiting beliefs, which are the major blocks to real growth and success in all areas of life.

Having used these methods to unlock great success in her own life, Sarah now shares these ground-breaking techniques with others.

Change yourself, Change your Beliefs, Change your life!

Contact Sarah:

Email:
sarah@sallyg.com
Website:
sallyg.com
Facebook Public:
facebook.com/sallygcoaching
Personal:
facebook.com/sarahgriffiths16144
Group:
facebook.com/groups/milldollarmindtribe/
Instagram:
instagram.com/sallygcoaching
LinkedIn:
linkedin.com/in/sarahgriffithssallyg/

MELISSA BROWN ODAZIE

Investor, Entrepreneur, Financial Advisor and Philanthropist

"Never lose your passion."

-Melissa Brown Odazie

Melissa Brown Odazie is a passionate entrepreneur, the CEO of her own company as well as sits on the board of several other firms, where she is able to apply her skills in the marketing, investing and financial sectors. Melissa works with various government tenders, leaders and organizations throughout the world, lending her expertise in commodities and trade both domestic and internationally as well as funding resources both traditional and non-traditional.

Melissa has been working as an Investor and advisor to her clients for over ten years bringing a wealth of knowledge from her background in Securities, Commercial Real Estate and as a Marketing and Communications Director. However, her heart is in Philanthropy and passionately pursues projects that have humanitarianism at the forefront.

In addition to being a licensed broker, Melissa has Her M.B.A. in Economics and International Business Studies, as well as an undergrad in marketing and Political Science.

Founder and Partner at Pyramid International Enterprises LLC Melissa continues to work with Entrepreneurs and Leaders around the world to pursue projects that she feels will make a positive and lasting impact for everyone.

Contact Melissa:

Website:
pyramidinternationalent.com
Email:
admin@pyramidinternationalent.com
Facebook Personal:
facebook.com/melissamilaodazie/
Facebook Business:
facebook.com/pyramidinternationalenterprisesllc/
Pinterest:
pinterest.com/queenmila4/
SkypeID:
Melissa Odazie
Live:
b0c71027e08c419

HAZEL TODD

Solicitor, Author and Entrepreneur

"Women are creators after all."

-Hazel Todd

Hazel Todd is a solicitor, admitted to practice law in Victoria, Australia. Before emigrating to Australia, she was admitted to practice in Botswana, having read for her law degree in South Africa. Though she was born in the UK, she grew up in Africa, having lived in Rhodesia (yep she's that old) later Zimbabwe, Botswana and South Africa.

She now runs her own practice, HazeLegal, dealing primarily in Wills and Estates, as well as family law.

When she is not working she enjoys writing, Latin and Ballroom dancing, and learning French. She lives in Melbourne with her three children and her little dog.

Her other works include:

'My life Manual: Estate Planning, Information and Messages for my Executors and Loved Ones – Australian Edition'

'My Life Manual: Estate Planning, Information and Messages for my Executors and Loved Ones – International Edition'

'The Dream Catcher: A Journal for Success'

'Powerful Conversations – 10 Stories of Authentic & Effective Conversations' (Co-author)

Contact Hazel:

Website:
the-life-manual.com
hmtodd.com
hazelegal.com.au
Facebook Public:
facebook.com/Hazelegal/
Facebook Personal:
facebook.com/hmtoddauthor/

VERONIKA WHYTE

Behavior Specialist, Educator and Author

"If it was easy, everyone would be successful."

-Veronika Whyte

Veronika Whyte is a practicing behavior specialist, educator and author. She has fifteen years of a proven track record of successful academic results in research of linguistics, education and psychology. She dedicated her interest to the study of crucial components of effective communication, which led Veronika to establish her own company Happy Beyond Limit, an international training and consulting company based on her body of research of psychology, communication and business skills.

In her chapter, you will learn the key principles and how to use them to become an authentic communicator to be able to hold powerful conversations in your business. It is perfect for the individuals who strive for personal success and expressing it through their business. These principles will move you toward profound personal change and act as a driving force to your success. For this journey, allow yourself the gift of time to experience the transformation you seek.

Contact Veronika:

Website:
happybeyondlimits.com
Facebook Public:
facebook.com/successbeyondlimits/
Instagram:
instagram.com/veronikawhyte/

United We Stand
Together We Soar

Lightning Source UK Ltd.
Milton Keynes UK
UKHW01f0019290918
329712UK00011B/1018/P